Counseling Principles for Christian Leaders

Counseling Principles for Christian Leaders

James A. Jones

QUALITY PUBLICATIONS
P.O. BOX 1060
ABII FNF, TEXAS 79604-1060

© James A. Jones 1982

Scripture quotations taken from the HOLY BIBLE: NEW INTERNATIONAL VERSION, copyright © 1978 by the New York International Bible Society. Used by permission of Zondervan Bible Publishers.

ISBN: 0-89137-534-1

TABLE OF CONTENTS

Chapter One
POOR, MOURNFUL AND MEEK – A PARADOX

Chapter Two
TRUTH – A BASIC HUMAN NEED

Chapter Three
MERCY AND PURITY – HEALING PRINCIPLES

Chapter Seven

ENCOURAGING AND COMFORTING THE BEREAVED

Chapter Eight

COUNSELING IS A UNIQUE RELATIONSHIP

Chapter Nine

COMMUNICATION – A MEANS OF GROWING SPIRITUALLY

AFFECTIONATELY DEDICATED
TO
MY FATHER AND MOTHER

My father taught me how to be proud, how to set structure and how to be firm. My mother taught me how to be tender and how to care. They both taught me how to persevere. Though they are dead, they speak clearly through me.

FOREWORD

I was honored and privileged to review the manuscript by Mr. James A . Jones entitled *Counseling Principles for Christian Leaders.*

His description of counseling techniques is sound. He writes in a clear fashion that can be appreciated by a broad range of ministers and mental health personnel. His sound counseling principles are well correlated with Scripture.

I would highly recommend Mr. Jones' manual of counseling techniques·not only for the ministry, but to mental health skeptics who can see no correlation between psychotherapeutic techniques and what was originally stated in the Scripture.

Lewis H. Lipsius, M.D.
Diplomate American National
Board of Psychiatry

ACKNOWLEDGEMENTS

I gratefully acknowledge that a number of individuals have influenced me in my professional development. I am thankful to each of my academic professors and clinical supervisors for what they have taught me. Although their influence is interwoven in this book, I take responsibility for its contents.

I acknowledge my gratitude to Nancy Browne, Dorothy Landers, Joan Scraggs, Barbara Walker, and Sherrel Wilson for typing, proofreading, and re-typing the number of revisions through which this material has come. To Lewis Lipsius, M.D., I express my gratitude for reading the manuscript and writing the foreword. I am also thankful to Virginia Richardson for the two pieces of art work which she did.

INTRODUCTION

Writing this book has forced me to come to grips with the pain as well as the joy of growing. It has come from my struggle with life's questions and problems and is especially written to those who struggle with the same. Therefore, I hope its contents will not be used as mere techniques, but will be assimiliated by those who are concerned and shared with those who are in need of care.

This book has grown out of my struggle to integrate theory and practice. It is the result of looking seriously at whether the Bible really speaks to man in his search for meaning and purpose while he is often experiencing the meaninglessness of his own experience.

This material is written for such leaders as ministers, elders, deacons, and Bible teachers. Leaders who have minimal or no professional training in counseling, but are nevertheless involved in counseling individuals who come to them for help with their many problems. Even though it is not written for professional psychotherapists, it is my hope that it would be of some value to them.

My primary purpose for this book is to establish that the beatitudes as recorded in Matthew 5:3-12 and other biblical passages contain principles of how to approach and solve intrapersonal and interpersonal problems to the extent possible. The material is not presented with the idea of being all conclusive, but with the desire to be accurate. I hope enough detail is given to assist the reader in both understanding the principles set forth herein and perceiving how to use them in solving problems. I have attempted to help Christian leaders see the interrelation of biblical principles to the ongoing problems of life.

One reason why Christian leaders need to be studying counseling critically and analytically is that it can be an effective teaching method. Counseling needs to be understood just as other methods,

13

such as the lecture or group discussion. Like other teaching methods, neither is it a panacea for individuals nor is every Christian ready for it.

Not everyone is an effective lecturer or group discussion leader; nor is everyone an effective counselor. The same teacher of the same students can be effective at times and ineffective at other times. Just as no teacher is prepared to teach every subject on every age level, no counselor is able to help everyone with all the problems he might have.

Traditional teaching and counseling are similar. Their effectiveness is based on the *teacher* (counselor – his interests, needs, level of development), and the *learning process.* Therefore, careful selection of a client or counselor should be made by a person.

Individuals tend to get involved in counseling others without first seriously considering whether they are personally suited for it or need to be educated in this field. I think a leader cannot be as effective as he is capable if he does not study counseling critically and practice it diligently and sagaciously. If religious leaders will not accept haphazard preparation and presentation of sermons and lessons by ministers and teachers, is it a mark of wisdom for them to accept such when it comes to their counseling? This is not intended to hurt any leader, but hopefully to challenge every leader who reads this book to rethink his thoughts about counseling and the type of job he is doing as a counselor. It seems to me that logic and wisdom force the serious leaders to conclude that he must take his counseling seriously and give it as much attention as he has given preaching, teaching Bible classes, visitation, personal evangelism, etc.

Inasmuch as leaders do counsel their followers (whether it is recognized or effective), it seems to me that they would be wise to develop some expertise in this area of their work. This is not to say that every leader can or should become a professional therapist. It is to say that, since so much of his work is involved in some type of counseling, being an effective counselor deserves his serious attention and adequate study.

James A. Jones
Atlanta, GA

14

Chapter 1

POOR, MOURNFUL AND MEEK – A PARADOX

PRINCIPLES IN PROBLEM SOLUTIONS

If the Bible is the word of God and, in fact, "useful for teaching, rebuking, correcting, and training in righteousness, so that the man of God may be thoroughly equipped for every good work,"[1] it follows that it should give insight into the solutions of personal and interpersonal problems. The Bible does speak to this matter numerous times, but perhaps in no place does it set forth greater clarity and thoroughness than in what is frequently called the Beatitudes.[2]

If the Beatitudes become the way an individual lives, they are of necessity the way he approaches and solves his problems. If the Beatitudes are the way a person lives and if problems are a part of living, then the Beatitudes are inherent in both his approach to and solution of his problems.

Often ministers and teachers have preached, lectured, and written on the Beatitudes with their focus being on "Happiness." Lewis said:

> The term "beatitude" comes from *beatitudo,* the Latin Bible's rendering of *makarios* (blessed) . . . . the beatitude is an interjection: "O, the happiness of!" or "Congratulations to!", but the happiness is in religious happiness and not delightful feelings.[3]

Although the word *blessed* does carry with it the idea of being happy, congratulated, or fortunate, individuals tend to think of happiness as being "play and laughter" and not equated with the appropriate and adequate solution of their problems. Persons who feel that happiness is playing and laughter may give "lip service" to applying the principles to their problems spasmodically and haphazardly; but when they become frustrated because "they did not work", they ignore them and try "something else" for a while. When the "something else" proves fruitless, they perhaps return to a casual consideration of the Beatitudes. Thus, their superficial, infrequent study and attempted application of the Beatitudes to the solution of their problems neither make real sense to them nor are helpful in improving their living. However, this does not prove that the Beatitudes do not give appropriate and adequate insight into how to solve one's problems. A consistent and continual practice of the Beatitudes is really learning how to live or be happy. It should be understood that a person *cannot be happy* (in the true sense of the term) without solving his problems. An individual who is in a continual process of solving his problems is not only happy, but is continually increasing his happiness.

Perhaps it would be wise for a person, while studying the Beatitudes, to keep in mind the following five suggestions:

1. Happiness is not laughing and having fun, although a happy person does laugh and have fun. There are many other reasons why an individual may laugh. Solomon said: "Even in laughter the heart may ache, and joy may end in grief."[4] He also stated: "Sorrow is better than laughter, because a sad face is good for the heart."[5]

2. *Makarios* **joy shines through tears.** Barclay's comment on happiness is helpful at this point. He says:

> *Makarios* describes the joy which has its secret within itself, that joy which is serene and untouchable, and self-contained, that joy which is completely independent of all the chances and changes in life. The English word *happiness* gives its own case away. It contains the root *hap,* which means *chance.* Human happiness is something which is dependent on the chances and changes of life, something which life may give and which life may also destroy . . . The Beatitudes speak of that joy which seeks us through our pain, that joy which sorrow and loss, and pain and grief, are powerless to touch, that joy which shines through tears and which nothing in life or death can take away.[6]

Paul and James speak of joy in this manner:

> We also rejoice in our sufferings, because we know that suffering produces perseverance; perseverance, character; and character, hope.[7]
>
> Consider it pure joy, my brothers, whenever you face trials of many kinds, because you know that the testing of your faith develops perseverance. Perseverance must finish its work so that you may be mature and complete, not lacking anything.[8]
>
> Blessed is the man who perseveres under trial, because when he has stood the test, he will receive the victor's crown, the life God has promised to those who love him.[9]

3. Due to the fact that our society is so pleasure-oriented and views happiness not in terms of inward dispositions, but outward circumstances (accumulation of wealth, education, position, or pleasure), perhaps it would be wise for one to **substitute the**

words *blessed* or *fortunate* for *happy* while studying the Beatitudes and when trying to apply them.

4. **The emphasis of one's study should be** *on the principles and not the promises.* Of the scores of individuals I have seen in therapy, the vast majority focused on the promises almost to the exclusion of principles. Perhaps one reason for this focus is that they did not understand that the Beatitudes were personal and interpersonal problem-solving principles.

5. **There are eight interrelated principles which should guide a person in solving his problems. These principles likely do not refer to eight different types of characters or persons, but to different characteristics of the same person.**[10] They should become so much a part of a person that they really describe different aspects of his character and become his natural way of attempting to solve any problem.

The better understanding one has of the principles, the longer he has been in process of digesting them, the more they have become a part of him, the easier it is for him to use them when approaching and solving a problem. Naturally, some problems are easier and quicker to solve then others. It is also true that some of the principles may be more pronounced than others in solving a given problem. To illustrate, a person may experience intense mourning in solving the problem of pregnancy out of marriage, but much less (comparatively speaking) in solving a problem of cheating on a daily exam. One will be much easier and quicker, but really to solve either will require an individual's utilization of the eight principles.

"BLESSED ARE THE POOR IN SPIRIT, FOR THEIRS IS THE KINGDOM OF HEAVEN."[11]

A counselor (elder, Bible teacher, minister, etc.) who approaches his and/or his client's problem as though he has the answers and does not recognize and accept his "poverty" will do little, if anything, constructive towards the solution of the problem. In fact, the "poverty principle" is the first principle to be applied in approaching and/or solving any problem. It is true that "pride goes before destruction, a haughty spirit before a fall."[12] It should also be understood that "when pride comes, then comes disgrace, but with humility comes wisdom."[13]

One of the reasons why many marital, family, and congregational problems are never solved (but many times get worse) is that individuals approach each other and their problems out of a spirit of arrogance and haughtiness. One way such feelings are manifested is through laughing and/or pretending that problems do not exist; or if they do, it is the other's fault. It would be wise indeed for each Christian to be aware that "if anyone thinks he is something when he is nothing, he deceives himself."[14] Jesus said: "Apart from me you can do nothing."[15] On the other hand, He said, "You are already clean because of the word I have spoken to you."[16] That being the case, if a Christian wants to be clean or solve his problems, he begins where the word begins — he is "poor in spirit."

This concept is contrary to what many believe. It may sound dehumanizing, but it (and the other principles) makes for personal development and not individual degradation. The more a person grows and is involved with individuals who are attempting to solve their problems, the clearer he perceives the reality of this principle. There is grace and hope for the individual who will swallow his pride and renounce his stubborn will.

Personal and physical poverty is something of which most individuals in our society are ashamed. Like any other problem of which one is ashamed, it must be faced and dealt with to be overcome. It is possible that the leader can vividly recall instances in which he had a personal, marital, family, or congregational problem but was too ashamed to admit genuinely his poverty to himself much less to someone else. Of course, a person may not have the "faintest idea" how to approach, much less solve, his problem. On the other hand, it is possible for an individual to act arrogantly and boastfully when responding to a particular problem as if to say he was the source of bounty himself.

Church leaders, spouses, and parents who have not discovered the richness of poverty likely are unmercifully sinning against themselves. It can be accurately stated that they are starving themselves to death. They have never discovered that possessing everything begins with having nothing. Notice what Paul said: "Sorrowful, yet always rejoicing; poor, yet making many rich; having nothing, and yet possessing everything."[17] Through the years individuals have said they thought they had everything, only to discover they had "nothing". Both spouses and parents have shared in therapy how they thought they had "perfect marriages and children" only to discover that they had let themselves believe a lie and were now in the throes of condemnation.

This concept of poverty is neither a pious phrase nor a lip-service ritual. It is a genuine recognition and acceptance of one's true condition.

18

"BLESSED ARE THOSE WHO MOURN FOR THEY SHALL BE COMFORTED."[18]

When a person truly faces his problem, genuine insight into his proverty leads him naturally into mourning although the degree and length of time involved will vary. Clear and analytical perception may reveal that an individual has thought or said: "I am rich; I have acquired wealth and do not need a thing. But you do not realize that you are wretched, pitiful, poor, blind and naked."[19] What is worse is that some individuals have discovered in therapy with me that they had this kind of attitude, yet had been repressed into their unconscious and were unaware of having it. They had not approached their problems out of their poverty, which would lead them to mourn and experience comfort, but out of arrogance, which led to more discomfort.

Mourning which grows out of facing the reality of who one is, what he has taught, said, and done is mourning which can bring comfort. It is the type of mourning which leads a person to change his mind, confess his error, ask for forgiveness, and seek reconciliation. It is not mourning which comes from having been "found out" or "caught".

If individuals are going to be successful in overcoming the world and really having abundant life, parents and teachers must help them to develop a realistic and adequate value system, clearly and precisely defined. A person cannot successfully live without a set of values, but if he is committed to a set of values which are unrealistic and inadequate, they will lead to internal conflicts. A well-defined, realistic and adequate value system, to which a person genuinely commits himself, will make for his health and wholeness. When he does not live up to it, he finds that his realistic guilt leads him to change his mind about a particular attitude or behavior. This enables him to forgive himself and the individual experiences cleansing, forgiveness, and reconciliation. In this context a person is truly fortunate or blessed when he mourns because he will be comforted.

Much emphasis in Bible classes and sermons is based on God's forgiving a person, but the greatest problem with reference to forgiveness lies initially with whether or not a person was reared in a forgiving environment. This eventually has a profound influence on whether or not an individual can forgive himself. If a child, being taught the truth on his developmental level, makes a mistake, is aided by his parents and teachers to see and accept his mistake, is forgiven by them and feels their forgiveness, he likely will come to

19

have an adequate scriptural value system which will enable him to forgive himself as often as is necessary. He would experience forgivenesss from others and himself and will have no serious difficulty with accepting the fact that God can forgive him of any sin of which he will confess and repent.

An experienced Christian counselor knows that forgiveness is only genuinely learned in the experience of ongoing relationships. A person who grew up in relationships where he was never forgiven likely will not forgive himself and others nor be able to accept God's forgivenesss without Christian professional help. To tell such a deprived individual that he has to forgive is at best wasting words and at worst contributing to serious psychological problems. A client, if helped, usually must be aided over a long period of time by his counselor and other significant individuals to learn how to forgive himself and others. Most of the time it will take a Christian therapy-type relationship for an individual to learn how to do this. What could have been initially a natural and relatively easy process will now likely be quite frightening, very painful, and time-consuming for the client.

Counseling is a relationship in which a person can learn something of how to forgive himself and experience forgiveness, reconciliation, and redemption. A function of counseling is to help a person discover and obey the truth in order to become free. This relates to the truth about himself and his relationship with God and others.

Perhaps one of the reasons why some leaders in the church have as much difficulty as they do in solving problems successfully is that they do not begin and continue with the "poverty principle" and operate out of a realistic, adequate, and clearly defined value system. One unrealistic concept to which some leaders subscribe is that the heart (emotions) is not an inherent part of personal and interpersonal problems. Such problems can never be solved until the emotional components are faced honestly and openly. Often some leaders try to solve such problems through ignoring and avoiding emotions like anger, fear, anxiety, rejection, isolation, loneliness, insecurity, inferiorness, disrespect, or unconcern.

The one emotion which is usually looked at is guilt. However, its dynamics are usually neglected and the focus gets more on who is guilty. As a result, forgiveness of self and others may seldom be genuinely experienced. The emotion of guilt needs to be looked into analytically. To illustrate:

Is the person showing evidence of values which are clearly defined.?

Is the individual dealing with specifics or generalities?

Is the individual showing evidence of forgiving himself or does he seem to feel more and more guilty?

Does he feel any shame?

After the problem theoretically has been solved, does the individual demonstrate that he has forgiven himself and others, or is there a cowered look on his face and in his posture?

Does he avoid others and is he losing interest in what used to be interesting to him, such as missing Bible classes or worship services which he used to attend regularly?

These are just some of the components which need to be looked into if guilt is dealt with therapeutically.

The teaching of guilt in the church has tended to be vague and general; therefore, many Christians have a generalized feeling of guilt and do not feel guilty about specific thoughts and actions. Leaders have not been successful in helping individual Christians learn to forgive themselves. They need to understand the dynamics of guilt; teach, preach, and counsel with individuals in ways that will enable them to develop a realistic and adequate value system which is precisely and clearly defined; and demonstrate in their relationships that they forgive their followers. It only complicates problems for an individual to confess publicly or privately that he has sinned, but cannot be specific about what sins he has committed. Furthermore, when an individual publicly states to those who are assembled that he has sinned, done wrong, or not set the right example in order to avoid confessing specifically to his mate, parent, brother or sister in Christ, he is only complicating his problem.

Another unrealistic value to which some leaders subscribe is that "big boys and men do not cry." This value causes many Christians to try to avoid their tears at almost any cost to themselves and their families. Notice how unscriptural this value is. "Jesus wept."[21] Individuals today may have thought He was having a nervous breakdown and that something terrible was happening to Him. Some people may not realize that crying can be an expression of love. Notice! "Then the Jews said, 'See how He loved him!' "[22]

The wise Teacher said, "There is a time for everything, and a season for every activity under heaven . . . a time to weep and a time to laugh."[23] One of the most beneficial things a person can do for himself is to experience his emotions in their seasons. Experiencing (working through) one's emotions is different from becoming emotional to get sympathetic attention in hopes of being taken care of or at least not being expected to be responsible for one's thoughts, feelings, and actions.

Still another unscriptural value which is rather widely taught in the church is if a person were a good Christian (whatever that means), he would not have any problems and, furthermore, it does not accomplish anything worthwhile to discuss them with someone else. This erroneous value causes considerable unnecessary conflict and pain in individuals and their relationships. Problems are inherent in being a person, being married, and growing up in one's family and congregation.

Counseling is a relationship in which a person can learn something of how to change the way he feels about his feelings and/or situation. Individuals tend to have far more difficulty with how they feel about their feelings than the feelings themselves. Although a person cannot change a basic emotion in the sense of eradicating it, he can change the way he feels about the emotion.

There are situations, though difficult, which can be changed and there are situations which cannot be changed. A function of counseling is to help a person look analytically at his situation with the hope of determining to what degree, if any, the situation cannot be changed by a client. He can learn how to change how he feels about the situation, learn to accept and live with it.

A person experiences more difficulty and less fulfillment avoiding, denying, blaming, accusing, and trying to get others to feel sorry for and take responsibility for him than he would if he would work through his resistance, accept, and learn to live with his reality. An individual may spend far more energy resisting the realities of his life than it would take to live with them if they were accepted and dealt with responsibly.

Life was designed by God to be fulfilling. Therefore, it is easier, more joyous and meaningful to have purpose in life than it is to "merely exist", run from, or fight living. Jesus said, "The thief comes only to steal and kill and destroy; I have come that they may have life, and have it to the full."[24]

"BLESSED ARE THE MEEK, FOR THEY WILL INHERIT THE EARTH."[25]

Many individuals defining meekness think of it as being spineless or lacking in courage. Both Moses and Jesus were meek, but who can say they lacked courage? Notice! "Now Moses was a very humble man, more humble than anyone else on the face of the earth."[26] Jesus stated, "Take my yoke upon you and learn from me, for I am gentle and humble in heart, and you will find rest for your souls."[27]

Aristotle saw meekness as being "the happy medium between too much and too little anger."[28] Therefore, one possible translation of this Beatitude is: "Blessed is the man who is always angry at the right time, and never angry at the wrong time."[29] The Teacher said, "There is a time to love and a time to hate."[30] Paul said, "In your anger do not sin: Do not let the sun go down while you are still angry, and do not give the devil a foothold."[31]

He who would solve his problems must learn to be aware of his anger and have the right amount at the right time for the right person. An effective counselor helps his client to become aware of his anger (as well as other feelings) and get it focused on the appropriate person and expressed at the appropriate time in the appropriate manner. This may require hours of teaching in counseling as well as in the classroom and from the pulpit. Unresolved, unrecognized, and displaced anger underlies most any personal, marital, or family problem.

The Greek word which is translated *meek* is also used to refer to an animal which has been trained or domesticated.[32] So, another possible translation of this Beatitude is: "Blessed is the man who has every instinct, every impulse, every passion under control. Blessed is the man who is entirely self-controlled."[33]

One of the goals a counselor should have is to aid the counselee in wanting to grow in self-control. A client may want to control his spouse, parents, or children, but may have little desire to control himself.

Paul said, "No, I beat my body and make it my slave so that after I have preached to others, I myself will not be disqualified for the prize."[34] Again, he states, "I have fought the good fight, I have finished the race, I have kept the faith."[35] When a counselee reaches the point where he is talking like this, he will be moving in the definite direction of solving his problems. Solomon said: "Better a patient man than a warrior, a man who controls his temper than one who takes a city."[36] He also states, "Like a city whose walls are broken down is a man who lacks self-control."[37]

A third possible way to approach this Beatitude is seeing that in meekness there is true humility. It should be understood that without humility a person cannot learn because the first step to learning is realizing one's own ignorance.[38] Therefore, a possible translation of this Beatitude is: "Blessed is the man who has the humility to know his ignorance, his own weakness, and his own need."[39]

Counseling is a relationship in which a person can learn something about his anger and how to deal with it constructively. Solomon said, "A gentle answer turns away wrath, but a harsh word stirs up anger."[40] An effective counselor neither confronts wrath with wrath nor denies or bypasses his counselee's anger. He does acknowledge his client's anger in an accepting manner and allows him to verbalize his wrath. He permits his counselee to vent his anger until he gets in control of himself (or to the point where the counselor feels his client could "hear" his response to him) and then focuses on the "pain" causing his anger. The primary focus is not on a client's anger, but on the underlying causes of it. A "gentle answer", and not "harsh words", is an appropriate and effective response to a counselee's anger because:

1. Counseling is not quarreling. Paul said: "And the Lord's servant must not quarrel; instead, he must be kind to everyone, able to teach, not resentful."[41]

2. Counseling is not a relationship in which **the counselor uses the counselee to vent his own frustrations, etc.**

3. Harsh words can stir up more anger.

4. Harsh words can cause one to "close up", not "open up".

5. Harsh words can cause one to want to deny and fight.

6. Gentle words communicate to a client that the counselor cares for him, is sensitive to his pain, and does not blame or condemn him for hurting.

7. Gentle words help a client lower his defenses and get in touch with his pain while wrath is a way of helping a client stay away from his pain.

8. Therefore, **gentle words help one to get where his basic problems are (inside himself).** It should be understood by a counselor that to the degree a person's problems are inside him to that degree is the solution found inside him.

24

FOOTNOTES

[1]2 Timothy 3:16,17.

[2]Matthew 5:3-12.

[3]Everett Ferguson, gen. ed., *The Living Word Commentary,* 19 vols. (Austin, Texas: Sweet Pub. Co., 1976), Vol. 2/1; Jack P. Lewis, *The Gospel According to Matthew,* (Austin, Texas: Sweet Pub. Co., 1976), p. 79.

[4]Proverbs 14:13.

[5]Ecclesiastes 7:3.

[6]William Barclay, *The Gospel of Matthew,* Vol. I (Philadelphia: The Westminster Press, 1975), p. 89.

[7]Romans 5:3,4.

[8]James 1:2-4.

[9]James 1:12.

[10]Lewis, *Gospel According to Matthew,* p. 79.

[11]Matthew 5:3.

[12]Proverbs 16:18.

[13]Proverbs 11:2.

[14]Galatians 6:3.

[15]John 15:5.

[16]John 15:3.

[17]2 Corinthians 6:10.

[18]Matthew 5:4.

[19]Revelation 3:17.

[20]2 Corinthians 7:10.

[21]John 11:35.

[22]John 11:36.

[23]Ecclesiastes 3:1,4.

[24]John 10:10.

[25]Matthew 5:5.

[26]Numbers 12:3.

[27]Matthew 11:29.

[28]Barclay, *Gospel of Matthew,* p. 96.

[29]*Ibid.*

[30]Ecclesiastes 3:8.

[31]Ephesians 4:26,27.

[32]Barclay, *Gospel of Matthew,* pp. 96, 97.

[33]*Ibid.,* p. 97.

[34]1 Corinthians 9:27.

[35]2 Timothy 4:7.

[36]Proverbs 16:32.

[37]Proverbs 25:28.
[38]Barclay, *Gospel of Matthew*, p. 97.
[39]*Ibid.*, p. 98.
[40]Proverbs 15:1.
[41]2 Timothy 2:24.

Chapter 2

TRUTH –
A BASIC HUMAN NEED

THE NEED TO DISCOVER AND ASSIMILATE

One of man's basic needs is to discover and assimiliate truth – the truth about who and what he is, where and with whom he does or does not fit, in what areas, and to what extent. A person cannot be truly satisfied or "filled" until he meets his need for truth on various levels at the time he needs it. Jesus said:

> If you hold to my teaching, you are really my disciples. Then you will know the truth, and the truth will set you free . . . So if the Son sets you free, you will be free indeed.[1]

Just as man gets confused about his other needs and how to meet them, so it is regarding his need to discover and assimilate truth. He tends to value his prejudices, limited knowledge, and traditions more than to have an open mind and a deep commitment to learning and digesting truth.

DIFFERENT METHODS OF DISCOVERING TRUTH

I accept Jesus Christ as truth[2] and the Bible as God's revelation of truth. I think there are different ways of discovering and experiencing the truthfulness of the Bible. Although there are different methods of discovering truth, it should be understood that truth remains truth, regardless of the method used to discover it.

A person's approach to and use of the Scriptures is based on his religious, psychological, and sociological background or experience. An individual's understanding of the Bible is based on his experience and there are various dimensions of a person's experience, such as psychological, sociological, and religious. Although this is true, it is possible for an individual to be unaware of the influence which his religious, psychological, and sociological past has on his study and use of the Scriptures. He may interpret what he is studying from his religious, psychological, and/or sociological past rather than from

27

the etymological meaning of the words and the context in which they appear. An individual should also understand that, if his awareness of himself and Scripture is incorrect, inadequate, and/or contradictory, his interpretation and use of Scripture will tend to be the same. A person should seek to be aware of himself and his past and differentiate these from what the Scripture itself says.

Perhaps the means used most frequently to discover truth by leaders in the church is the propositional method which is valid and effective. When used sagaciously, this method helps to bring out truth in a clearer and more specific way. It is invaluable to the truth seeker. The propositional method also forces an individual to think in clear, logical, and non-contradictory ways and should be utilized frequently in Bible classes and from the pulpit. This method, when used correctly, would help prevent error from being taught and accepted.

A precisely defined proposition does not necessarily include all truth on a particular subject nor other truths not included in the specific proposition. To illustrate, Jesus said, "I tell you no! But unless you repent, you too will all perish."[3] This very clearly states that repentance is necessary in order to be saved, but it does not give all the truth about repentance. Even though the Bible clearly teaches faith, confession, and baptism are necessary for salvation, this Scripture does not mention them. To have a clear understanding of what the Bible teaches on a particular subject, one must study it in its immediate and broader context wherever it appears in Scripture. Otherwise, a person may "force" a verse to teach that which it does not.

SYMBOLS – AN AVENUE TO TRUTH

A skilled counselor is aware that truth can be discovered through methods other than the propositional one. In trying to discover truth for himself as well as helping his client discover truth, a wise counselor learns from Jesus' usage of symbols. He was very skilled in the use of symbols or figures of speech. He frequently used similes *as* and *like,* metaphors, and parables to teach individuals the truth. An effective Christian counselor, using Christ as a model, finds himself often using "that sounds like . . . " or "you talk as though . . . ." An effective counselor not only understands symbolic language, but often speaks it. He knows that symbolic language is a key through which his client may be able to discover more truth about himself, God, and others. He can also understand the truth he already knows in a clearer and more specific manner as he grows in his understanding and wise use of symbolic language himself. He who would be effective in counseling must be able to think in terms of symbols — clearly understanding and skillfully using them. A literalist is very limited in being able to help another person with his problems.

Symbols are necessary to the discovery of and participation in truth. Symbols can penetrate a person's defenses and open him up to truths about which he is blind. A symbol can be less threatening to an individual than direct confrontation.

If a symbol continues to have significant meaning in a person's life, it must lead him to truth about himself and his relationships as well as to broader or more comprehensive reality. If a symbol does not lead one to specific truth, then the use of that symbol loses its meaning and power in an individual's life. The more symbols a person uses superficially and thoughtlessly, the less power they will have in his life and the emptier his life will become.

Most of the power a symbol has for a person likely is not utilized while he is in the actual participation of the symbol. This is not to say that an individual should not use a symbol or should use it less, but it simply acknowledges the nature of symbols and a person's use of them. Likely, the greatest power a symbol has for an individual is during a crisis in his life; due to other circumstances he is more open, receptive, and reflective to its meaning and power in his life and relationships.

One of the problems with symbols is that a person may use them out of custom and conformity, not out of insight into their meanings and individual commitment to using them. A person may have had some insight into the meaning of a symbol, but did not cultivate his perception. Therefore, when crises have come, he was unable to use the symbol to meet his needs on a deeper level.

Unless symbols grow out of and relate to a person's experience, they have little to no meaning and impact in his life. During the process of one's growth, a symbol will take on different shades of meaning at various times. Through experience a symbol can have additional and deeper meanings for a person, yet he may expect a symbol to have the same meanings for another as it does for him. Symbols can also have unconscious meanings for a person.

ONE'S THOUGHTS AND FEELINGS CHANGE

Some individuals are of the opinion that a person cannot trust (depend on) his feelings because they change. If one's feelings cannot be trusted because they change, then his thoughts cannot be trusted because they change, too. The truth of the matter was stated by Jeremiah when he said: "I know, O Lord, that a man's life is not his own; it is not for man to direct his steps."[4] Therefore, a person needs an objective standard by which to live. For the Christian, that standard is the Bible.

God created man with several emotions or feelings and he can think about as well as feel more than one of them at one time. Often a person experiences ambivalence; i.e., he feels both negative and positive feelings at once. For example, an individual can have feelings of "like" and "anger" at the same time. One potential problem each person has in dealing with his feelings is that not only can he avoid his feelings or deny them, but he can be aware of and deal with only one or part of his feelings to the exclusion of other feelings. This is frequently done with anger. Many individuals have serious difficulty in recognizing, accepting, and explicitly verbalizing their anger. Of the ones who verbalize their anger, a large percentage are not aware of and do not share the primary feelings which cause them to feel anger.

Anger is a secondary feeling caused by other feelings. A person will never be able to deal effectively (therapeutically) with his anger until he can simultaneously deal with the feelings causing his anger. In fact, once a person can recognize, accept, and explicitly verbalize his anger (in a non-condemning, attacking, and defensive manner), most of his time, emotional energy and thoughts should be focused on recognizing, accepting, and precisely sharing his feelings which cause his anger.

I do not propose to know all the reasons why individuals have problems with their emotions, but some are:

1. Their "minds" have been educated, but their "hearts" (emotions) have been denied or avoided. Not being aware, much less understanding, and not having years in which to experience their emotions naturally, they have been educated (verbally and nonverbally) to feel ashamed, afraid, and/or guilty about their feelings.

2. Likely they have been taught something about thinking, but not feeling. Intrapersonal and interpersonal counseling tends to teach individuals something about how to think and feel.

A person can learn how to think without feeling, but an individual cannot learn how to feel and express his emotions respectfully and responsibly without thinking. Thinking without feeling leads to extremes in thoughts, feelings, and behaviors in a similar way as feeling without thinking does. In fact, he who goes to extremes is one who thinks without feeling or feels without thinking.

30

3. They repress and/or suppress their feelings. Many Christians have been educated to believe that if they are not aware of their feelings they do not have feelings. They do not understand that repression and/or suppression of their feelings does not get rid of them — it only guarantees that they will be expressed in disguised ways, which most likely will be confusing, frustrating, and unhealthy for the individual and his relationships.

Very few teenagers have sexual intercourse primarily for meeting their sexual needs. Neither are they ignorant of biological and physiological facts nor oversexed. A teenage girl may become promiscuous sexually as a way of expressing her need for affection or self-worth, or because she is angry.

An individual may engage in promiscuous sexual relationships because of:

a. A desire for love and affection.

b. Rebellion against authority or a domineering mother or father — possessiveness and unhealthy tyranny of one of his parents.

c. Dependence, greed, hate, hostility, retaliation, and revenge.

d. Feeling the need to prove his social acceptability or impress his friends.

e. Reassurance as to one's masculinity or femininity.

f. An attempt to prove one's self-superiority.

A teenager may feel worried about the possibility of his parents getting a divorce and "break the law" with the hope (possibly unconscious) his parents will get some help with their marriage. A child may sometimes act out in his family as a way of saying he is worried about his parents.

It is true that feelings change, but so do thoughts. One can no more rely on his feelings than he can his thoughts. A person can have a psychotic episode or "leave the church" over his thoughts as well as his feelings. In fact, in many cases unrecognized and unresolved feelings contribute largely to his psychotic break and/or "leaving the church". To illustrate, a philosophy teacher may upset a Christian student by presenting different thoughts and ideas. However, a student who knows how to think analytically, has a healthy self-respect, and is not filled with feelings of inferiority, worthlessness, shame, guilt, and contradictions in his value system likely is going to become stronger through the experience rather than disbelieving God and "quitting the church."

One of the serious questions facing Christian educators is whether or not they are teaching their students how to think analytically and critically as well as genuinely feel. Leaders need to understand that a faith which is unquestioned or not examined is a faith of little substance. Neither thoughts nor feelings are to be trusted unless they are built on a sound, adequate, and realistic value system (standard). For me, the basis of a person's value system should be the Bible – not what he has heard, been taught, always believed, and thinks he knows–but the Bible.

Appropriate use of Scripture in counseling is in the context of the relationship. Jesus did not begin with a "text and preach from it". He began with an individual – where he was, and not where He wanted him to be. Christ began with a person's need and then helped the individual to see how Scripture could help him meet his need. Jesus' use of Scripture was in part to help a person see that Scripture applied to his particular problems and specific questions. Christ understood that a person hears and speaks in his own frame of reference; therefore, He spoke in it when addressing a particular individual. Christ used Scripture after He got into a person's frame of reference, not before. He did not arbitrarily begin with Scripture and hope the person would and could apply it to himself and his life in a meaningful way.

Counseling is a relationship in which a client has a right to become aware of, understand, and verbally express any and all of his emotions. It is a relationship in which a counselee can "talk about", but not "act out" his emotions.

"BLESSED ARE THOSE WHO HUNGER AND THIRST FOR RIGHTEOUSNESS, FOR THEY WILL BE FILLED."[5]

Two of the most powerful drives known to man were used by Christ to indicate the intensity with which a person should crave righteousness. A possible translation of this Beatitude is: "Blessed are those who hunger and thirst for the whole of righteousness, for complete righteousness."[6] So many individuals are "hung up" on "who is right" instead of "what is right". Many of those who are searching for what is right do so only half-heartedly and therefore, are never filled or satisfied. Another mistake made by many people is that they focus on the "goal" instead of the "means". Realistic goal setting is necessary for the solution of problems, answering of questions, and growth. Once a goal is set, the maturing individual focuses on the means (process) to the goal and not the goal itself.

Counseling is not trying to decide who is right, joining sides with him, and condemning the other person although a counselor is tempted at times to do so. Solomon said, "The first to present his case seems right, till another comes forward and questions him."[7] Paul should be taken seriously when he said, "Be careful to do what is right in the sight of everybody."[8] An effective counselor is in search of the truth concerning what is going on, not who is right or wrong.

Counseling is a relationship in which a person can learn something about relationships. An assumption of mine is that this understanding can help a person move in the direction of what is right in his relationships. I think of relationships as having three general phases which are interwoven and do overlap. The stages or phases are "honeymoon", disappointment, and reality. The "honeymoon" stage is filled with romanticism and idealism. It is thinking that the relationship is and will be perfect. It is the stage in which individuals feel that magic and miracles happen.

The disappointment phase is becoming aware of the fact that one did not get the ideal spouse, child, congregation, minister, counselor, and that there are no magic or miracles. *This is a critical stage in marriage, family, counseling, and congregational relationships.* It is in this stage that couples divorce; children are abandoned or run away from home; Christians tend to "quit" the church; ministers leave the ministry; elders, deacons, and teachers resign; and counselees stop coming for counseling.

The reality phase of relationships is that phase in which the ideal has been given up, the disappointment worked through, and individuals begin to accept themselves and each other for what they are, not for what they thought they were, wished they were, or need them to be. It is the phase in which "magic" and "miracles" have been discarded and the individual is willing to be responsibly involved in an open, honest, respectful, and persevering relationship. It is the phase in which an individual understands that no one else has his answers for him and he is not looking for a quick solution or a pious answer. Instead, he is willing to discover the principles God has set forth in His word, not desiring to "arrive", but always being in the process of becoming more like Christ. It is that phase in which a person realizes that there is sin in the best individual and good in the worst, but he is deeply committed to dealing with both the good and the bad in himself as well as others. It is seeing and accepting himself as the sinner he is, but realizing that by God's grace and through his faith there is always hope and potential. This is that phase in which an individual learns that joy comes from suffering, struggling, and pain. It is understanding that there are valleys and peaks in everyone's life and, rather than denying or resisting, he is willing to go through the valley and climb the mountain to reach its peak once again.

It is sad, but nevertheless true, that there are Christians who never experience the depth of meaning and joy in the reality phase of relationships. They end their marriages, give up on their children, and "quit" the church. Some people spend their lives running, "being tossed to and fro and carried about with every wind of doctrine", looking for the "honeymoon" of life. Never finding the "honeymoon" or working through their disappointment, they continue to drift and meander around in life without meaning and purpose and are ready and willing to jump on any pious statement or quick solution to their problem.

Counseling, especially long term, can enable a person to come to grips with his disappointments with relationships, work through those disappointments, and learn how to be involved creatively in the realistic phase of relationships. One limitation of brief counseling is that it cannot help a client deal very thoroughly with this important aspect of relationships.

One focus of an effective counselor is helping individuals to discover what relationship phase they are in. Once this is established, a skilled counselor helps the individuals to focus on the dynamics in that phase in terms of what their needs are. Hungering and thirsting for righteousness is a basic therapeutic principle. If used sagaciously, it can help individuals solve their problems and heal their wounds.

Counseling is using knowledge wisely, not taking sides with a particular counselee. Solomon said: "A gentle answer turns away wrath, but a harsh word stirs up anger."[9] He also stated, "The tongue that brings healing is a tree of life, but a deceitful tongue crushes the spirit."[10]

An effective counselor considers carefully what he hears as well as how he is listening. Jesus said, "Consider carefully what you hear."[11] Solomon states, "A simple man believes anything, but a prudent man gives thought to his steps."[12] Again, he states, "He who answers before listening – that is his folly and shame."[13] Again, "A fool's lips bring him strife, and his mouth invites a beating. A fool's mouth is his undoing, and his lips are a snare to his soul."[14] But, "An honest answer is like a kiss on the lips."[15] A counselor needs to realize that "a gentle tongue can break a bone."[16] Furthermore, a counselor needs to take Jesus seriously when He said, "Therefore, consider carefully how you listen."[17]

Solomon said, "Do not answer a fool according to his folly, or you will be like him yourself. Answer a fool according to his folly, or he will be wise in his own eyes."[18] It is relatively easy to see why a person would not answer a fool according to his own folly lest he be like him, but a wise individual naturally wonders what value there is in answering a fool according to this own folly. There are several reasons why the skilled counselor would answer according to his client's folly.

1. To penetrate his defenses. If a client is asking for help, but continues to resist help and will not respond to a counselor's attempt to analyze the resistance, answering him according to his own folly may be an effective approach in penetrating his defenses. This type of response tends to be shocking and will often penetrate his defenses when other approaches fail.

2. To demonstrate the absurdity of his position, statement, or idea. This response not only tends to be shocking; but being able to hear, feel, and see his folly stated in a terse way by his counselor tends to free the client up enough to begin to see his absurdity when demonstrated by someone else.

3. To increase the counselee's level of awareness. Often in counseling, clients demonstrate their lack of awareness in various areas of their person as well as the manner in which they relate to others. Since a counselee's defenses are up and he cannot really see himself and the way he comes across the others, answering him according to his folly can be effective in helping him see the way he is. Obviously, this is a powerful way of responding to another person, especially one who is in a dependent relationship. A counselor should certainly seek to be "as shrewd as snakes and as innocent as doves"[19] when he is using this method of responding to his client.

Answering a client according to his folly implies, among other things, that the counselor is in control of himself as well as the relationship and has a rather clear perception of his client and how he is coming across to him.

A counselor can answer his client according to his own folly and the response likely will be therapeutic if:

1. He exercises clear self-awareness, self-control, self-respect, and self-confidence.

2. He has established an appropriate and adequate structure or contract.

3. He perceives sufficient strength in his client and their relationship.

An effective counselor carefully weighs what a client is saying in conjunction with how he is hearing his client. Analyses of both the "what" and "how" are determinants in "how", "when", and "with what" a counselor will respond to his counselee. He listens to understand instead of answering him. An appropriate answer or response tends to emerge naturally out of clearly perceiving what his client is sharing verbally and nonverbally.

A skilled counselor is aware of and intentionally responds to his clients nonverbally. He makes appropriate and skilled use of his eyes, gestures, posture, etc. Notice what Mark said of Jesus: "He looked around at them in anger."[20] He also would sit down, open His mouth, mark on the ground, have a child sit in His lap, etc.

Depending upon the strength of the counselee, what he wants from the counselor, and the nature and strength of the counseling relationship, an effective counselor reproves, rebukes, and exhorts with long-suffering when it is appropriate. Although this is a dynamic way of responding to an individual, Solomon points out its dangers and potentials. He said, "Better is open rebuke than hidden love."[21] Again, "Whoever corrects a mocker brings on insult; whoever rebukes a wicked man incurs abuse. Do not rebuke a mocker or he will hate you; rebuke a wise man and he will love you."[22]

A counselor's reproving, rebuking, or exhorting should be brief and with long-suffering. He needs to be aware of the fact that he cares about his client (if he does) and understands the difference between reproving, rebuking, or exhorting and condemning, blaming, or accusing. Furthermore, he should be alert to the overtones of his responses. A counselor needs to grow to the point where he can speak the truth in love. This type of responding to a client most often will come after a relationship is well-established. Even then, rebuking will not be a "steady diet" which the counselor tries to feed his counselee. In addition, reproving, rebuking, and exhorting in counseling should be one-sentence or one-question responses, not sermons or sermonettes. Jesus said, "Simply let your 'Yes' be 'Yes', and your 'No', 'No', anything beyond this comes from the evil one."[23]

Rather than concentrating on just "what to say" or "the right answer to give", Paul acknowledges that there are other matters to take into consideration. "Let your conversation be always full of grace, seasoned with salt, so that you may know how to answer everyone."[24] Paul says in this passage that there are two powerful forces which need to be taken seriously and from which one's answers to people should come. A counselor's conversation should be full of *grace* and seasoned with *salt*. If a counselor is really in touch with the reasons he feels that his conversation is full of favor

36

towards his client and filled with salt and if his reasons actually are valid, the appropriate response or answer naturally emerges. This is not to say that this process is easy to learn; but based on my experience, I can say that this theory is valid, not just because this is a verse of Scripture, but because I have seen it clinically demonstrated.

In addition, an effective counselor responds gently, kindly, tenderheartedly, and forgivingly. Solomon said, "A gentle answer turns away wrath, but a harsh word stirs up anger."[25] Paul said, "Be kind and compassionate to one another, forgiving each other, just as in Christ God forgave you."[26] Solomon affirmed that "a kind man benefits himself, but a cruel man brings himself harm."[27]

In the search for righteousness, the counseling relationship becomes one in which a client experiences appropriate judgment. In Scripture, judgment is not condemnation; it is not one person's siding against another. It is looking into and discerning the interrelation of the components of a given interchange, problem, question, or situation in light of its roots and broader context. It is an appropriate and precise response to a client out of this insight. Judgment is clearly taught in the Scriptures. A maturing counselor takes Jesus and Solomon seriously when they said:

> Do not judge, or you too will be judged. For in the same way you judge others, you will be judged, and with the measure you use it, it will be measured to you. Why do you look at the speck of sawdust in your brother's eye and pay no at- take the speck out of your eye," when all the time there is a plank in your own eye? You hypocrite, first take the plank out of your own eye, then you will see clearly to remove the speck from your brother's eye.[28]
> see clearly to remove the speck from you brother's eye.[28]
> Stop judging by mere appearances, and make a right judgment.[29]
> You judge by human standards; I pass judgment on no one. But if I do judge, my decisions are right, because I am not alone. I stand with the Father who sent me.[30]
> My son, preserve sound judgment and discernment, do not let them out of your sight; they will be life for you, an ornament to grace your neck.[31]

Hungering and thirsting for righteousness (what is right, appropriate, etc.) is a principle in problem solutions which is deeply valued by a skilled counselor. It is a principle by which an effective counselor faces his problems and helps his clients to do likewise.

FOOTNOTES

[1]John 8:31, 32, 36.
[2]John 14:6.
[3]Luke 13:3.
[4]Jeremiah 10:23.
[5]Matthew 5:6.
[6]Barclay, p. 101.
[7]Proverbs 18:17.
[8]Romans 12:17.
[9]Proverbs 15:1.
[10]Proverbs 15:4.
[11]Mark 4:24.
[12]Proverbs 14:15.
[13]Proverbs 18:13.
[14]Proverbs 18:6, 7.
[15]Proverbs 24:26.
[16]Proverbs 25:15.
[17]Luke 8:18.
[18]Proverbs 26:4, 5.
[19]Matthew 10:16.
[20]Mark 3:5.
[21]Proverbs 27:5.
[22]Proverbs 9:7, 8.
[23]Matthew 5:37.
[24]Colossians 4:6.
[25]Proverbs 15:1.
[26]Ephesians 4:32.
[27]Proverbs 11:17.
[28]Matthew 7:1-5.
[29]John 7:24.
[30]John 8:15, 16.
[31]Proverbs 3:21, 22.

Chapter 3

MERCY AND PURITY – HEALING PRINCIPLES

BLESSED ARE THE MERCIFUL, FOR THEY WILL BE SHOWN MERCY.[1]

The word *mercy* means "the ability to get right inside the other person's skin until we can see things with his eyes, think things with his mind, and feel things with his feelings."[2] The person who shows mercy is the person who can relate to another *out of himself* – not outside himself. Individuals tend to "not make the deliberate effort to get inside the other person's mind and heart, until they see and feel things as he sees and feels them."[3] Being able to show mercy enables a person to be kind in the appropriate manner, not "slurpy sweet", "super nice" or flattering. Forgiveness and tolerance are not only possible, but are easier to achieve when mercy permeates a relationship.

Mercy is related to empathy. To empathize with one is to feel what the other feels from his internal frame of reference. If one has empathic understanding, he senses the feelings and personal meanings of the other person from the inside as they seem to him. It is trying to grasp clearly the meanings, feelings, and thoughts which the other person is trying to convey. It involves understanding pertinent facts, but equally important is how the person feels about himself, his experiences, and problems.

MAN NEEDS TO BE RELATED

Man needs to be related to others intellectually, emotionally, and spiritually on different levels at various times depending upon his and the other person's needs and availablity at a particular time. It is impossible to be related emotionally, intellectually, and religiously on every· level (from surface to depth) continually with oneself, much less anyone else, *even one's marriage partner.* Theoretically, a spouse may be related to his partner in more areas, at greater

39

depths, for longer periods of time than any other person. But, even when spouses are relating at their maximum, there is still the need in everyday life for them to be related to other individuals intellectually, emotionally, and spiritually. Counseling can be a relationship in which a person can learn how to relate to others on these levels.

One of man's basic needs is to have intimate interpersonal relationships. It is largely from one's relationships, especially his early ones, that he derives a sense of meaning and purpose in life, which is another basic need.

It is an established fact that the group to which a person belongs has a major influence on his perceptions, feelings, and actions. The group influences may be destructive or edifying to an individual; this depends on such factors as:

1. The nature of the group.

2. The purposes and goals of the group and the means to achieve them. These may be specific and clear or very ambiguous to the members of the group.

3. The underlying, motivating factors. Why did the person choose this group instead of another, or did he?

4. His extent of self-disclosure and depth of participation within the group.

5. The length of time he was a member of the group as compared to the length and degree of countering influences; for example, a 15-year-old child who spends one hour in Bible class and the rest of the week in a family and/or peer groups whose goals are basically different from his Bible teacher's.

6. His age and what kind of experiences he had before entering the group.

The following passages speak to group dynamics and should be taken seriously:

> My son, if sinners entice you, do not give in to them.[4]
> Do not be misled: "Bad company corrupts good character."[5]
> Therefore, encourage one another and build each other up, just as in fact you are doing.[6]
> And let us consider how we may spur one another on toward love and good deeds. Let us not give up meeting together, as some are in the habit of doing, but let us encourage one another — and all the more as you see the Day approaching.[7]

The Bible is replete with passages which emphasize the fact that parents are to nurture, educate, and train their children. I think Christian leaders should emphasize this basic responsibility of parents. However, the church's role in assisting parents in nurturing their marriage and the members of the family should not be minimized.

The Wise Man said, "Train a child in the way he should go, and when he is old he will not turn from it."[9] One of the questions which immediately comes to mind is, "What does it mean to train a child?" Does it mean that he is to be trained intellectually, emotionally, socially, religiously? Are each of these areas significant? Can he be a balanced individual if one or more of these areas are significantly lacking in his training? Are these areas interrelated and can one be trained in each of them simultaneously? If the areas overlap or are interwoven, would it be possible for a person to learn a religious concept effectively through being involved in some activity intellectually, emotionally, and behaviorally?

It seems to me that the most effective training for a child is that which involves the head, heart, and body simultaneously and deals consistently and adequately with his basic interests and needs in the midst of living. If this assumption is accurate, then the lecture method, or pulpit speaking, is not sufficient in and of itself. Also, if this assumption has validity, assembling four hours or three times a week is not sufficient, especially when two of the hours are not really for the child. This time may not be enough to counteract the training the child is receiving at home and in society, much less help him move in the appropriate direction.

It is important that a child learn Biblical facts, but it is equally important that they be presented to him in proper perspective. Biblical facts thoroughly furnish a child unto everything that is good. He needs to know the Biblical facts regarding the plan of salvation, the nature and worship of the church, etc.; but if he is to be trained effectively, he also needs to know the Biblical facts regarding how to live and not be overcome by a real and sometimes unfair evil world. Further, although a student may have correct and adequate facts, unless those facts are assimilated into this life, they will be of minimal value to him. Leadership in the church in times past has given considerable attention to Biblical facts being learned intellectually. However, there needs to be adequate attention given to how a child may be taught these facts in a way that they not only get into his head, but find lodging in his heart to bring about redemption, forgiveness, reconciliation, and wholeness of person and life.

If parents and other Christian leaders take seriously their responsibility to train, they should critically analyze their assumptions about training. Leaders should not be overcome with fear when their assumptions are challenged; though anxious, they should welcome such challenges. Just because leaders have held to certain assumptions about training does not in any way prove that the assumptions are accurate. The accuracy of an assumption is not validated by length of practice. A child is not necessarily being trained just because:

1. He is physically present. Being physically present for Bible class, etc., in no way proves that a child is learning what the teacher or parents would have him learn. While it is true that a child has to be physically present to learn, he may be learning the opposite of that which the leader would have him learn.

2. His being "talked to" does not necessarily mean that he is being trained correctly. Sometimes parents, Bible teachers, and ministers alike seem to feel that talking to a child is training him. There is a vast difference in talking to a child and getting him involved in a learning process. Although the one doing the talking may be presenting Biblical facts in their proper context and with zeal, a child may not even be listening, much less learning what is being said.

3. His being in a lecture class does not mean that he is being properly trained. One of the disadvantages of the lecture method is that often little learning may actually be taking place on the part of the students. This is not to say that a lecture may not be well prepared and logically presented. The lecturer may not be able to communicate effectively because the student does not understand, is not interested, or does not see the need of learning.

4. He may be only getting facts and understanding them on an intellectual level. Much teaching in the church consists of presenting facts with little to no effort made to help the student assimilate these facts. Therefore, a student may know many biblical facts and still not be trained in the ways of the Lord.

Effective training involves having an adequate and realistic set of doctrines, which are consistently taught verbally and nonverbally, explicitly and implicity in and out of the classroom. The Bible is that set of doctrines; but what Christians teach does not always harmonize with Scripture. Biblical teaching is often not comprehensive enough; nor is it taught frequently enough in appropriate educational settings. For example, marriage and family living and character development are often approached infrequently, ambiguously, and in over-simplistic terms as compared to the plan of salvation, the nature, organization, and worship of the church, which are frequently taught in clearer and more precise terms.

Another related basic need of man is a loving, trusting relationship with God. This relationship comes from and remains related to the type of interpersonal relationships one had early in his life and continues to have. The most religious-minded adults were reared by parents who themselves were deeply religious. Paul said, "I have been reminded of your sincere faith, which first lived in your grandmother Lois and in your mother Eunice, and I am persuaded, now lives in you also."[10]

It should be understood that children need parents and religious leaders who themselves are appropriate models. Otherwise, they can expect children to grow up using their religion in an unhealthy manner. Many religious ideas are taught from a negative, legalistic, and rigid point of view — creating distrust and resentment in youth and contributing to serious emotional and mental problems in various age groups. A leader needs to understand that any idea is strong only if it is grounded in a person's character structure. Two basic questions teachers and parents need to consider are:

1. Is what the child believes true?
2. Does the child believe it wholeheartedly?

FOCUS IN COUNSELING IS MORE ON SHAME THAN GUILT.

One of the functions of counseling is to help a person experience mercy appropriately. A means by which this can be done is focusing on a persons' shame dynamic and not his guilt dynamic. This does not mean that guilt is not important and should not be dealt with by an individual. In the counseling relationship, guilt likely will not be dealt with therapeutically unless it is done through the shame dynamic. In other words, just getting a person to talk about his guilt and feeling guilty is probably of little therapeutic value in the long run.

Guilt is more a state of mind — more what a person does or does not do and, at best, does not center on the person himself, but rather on his actions. It is relatively easy for most individuals to separate their actions from who they are as persons and see their actions as the totality of their being.

Focusing on the shame dynamic is an attempt to help a person see himself the way he is as well as what he does. This is a complicated and time-consuming process, but once a person sees himself for who he is, clearly perceives what he does, and openly accounts to himself and others (including God), he feels appropriate guilt because in reality he is a sinner. Focusing on a person's shame dynamic does not move a person away from his guilt, but to his guilt with a clearer understanding of what and why he is guilty. Furthermore, this focus makes a person's guilt specific, not vague and general. One of the serious problems in the church is that, for too long, leaders have operated out of the guilt dynamic to the exclusion of the shame dynamic. As a result, sitting in Bible classes and on the pews every week are numerous Christians who are feeling extremely guilty instead of experiencing forgiveness, redemption, reconciliation, peace and joy. It is a clinical fact that large numbers of Christians struggle with the nagging pain of chronic guilt.

Focusing on a person's shame begins and continues with looking to see what *is* and neither assuming innocence nor guilt. As a rule, focusing on the guilt dynamic begins and continues with the assumption that the client is automatically guilty. A skilled Christian counselor looks to see what *is* and attempts to deal with it. He does not relate to people to prove their innocence or guilt either to himself or to them.

Focusing on the shame dynamic gets at truth (which frees) while guilt tends to focus on who is guilty and to what extent. Therefore, it has a certain built-in bias, which is easy to get in one's way of growth. A Christian counselor who operates out of the guilt dynamic tends to see everything as "right or wrong", "good or bad", "black or white". The fact of the matter is there are definite "rights and wrongs", "blacks and whites", but most of the situations with which a Christian counselor deals are "grays" or "mixtures". In addition to this, my experience has been that most of the conflicts which couples and families have are psychological and sociological conflicts, which in and of themselves are neither moral nor immoral.

A person needs principles by which to live. Focusing on the guilt dynamic tends to lead to rule-keeping and a lack of joy and fulfillment in life. This happens because an individual tries to hide and cover himself rather than expose himself to who he is, as well as what he can become. The shame dynamic helps a person to see himself and his potential and assimilate principles (truth) which enables him to be free, happy, and whole.

LISTEN TO UNDERSTAND – NOT TO ANSWER

Another means of helping a person experience mercy is for a counselor to listen – not to answer, but to understand. Intrapersonal and interpersonal counseling is not listening to another for a few minutes to point out through a detailed analysis of what he said

44

wherein he is illogical or wrong. Such would likely be appropriate for an academic, legal, or financial advisor to do.

One of the serious mistakes that can be made in counseling is for a counselor to have the opinion that he must answer everything that is shared by a counselee. If he is of this opinion, he will likely be spending his time trying to figure out an answer and never really hear what the question is or even if there is a question. An individual who comes to counseling does not necessarily have questions he wants answered; nor does he have questions every session. A counselee may need to have someone with whom he can share his pain. On occasions, clients just have something to share and really do not want even as much as a verbal response from the counselor. Solomon can be helpful at this point:

> A fool finds no pleasure in understanding, but delights in airing his own opinion.[11]

> He who answers before listening – that is his folly and his shame.[12]

"OVERHEARD" CONVERSATION IS A MEANS OF EXPERIENCING MERCY.

Mercy can also be experienced through listening to another reveal himself. This is especially true in marriage, family, and group counseling. "Overheard" conversation has a potential learning level that is different and deeper than direct conversation. This is because of several reasons:

1. It is less threatening and embarrassing.
2. It is easier for one to listen to another, as a rule, when he is talking to someone else about how he feels and what he thinks.
3. Defenses are not as high.

Essentially the same reasons could be given as to why mercy can be experienced through talking to a counselor while others are listening. In fact, a skilled counselor requires that his counselees speak directly to him rather than one another most of the time. The assumption is that while a counselee and counselor are sharing in the ongoing experience of therapy, the others are being given an opportunity to see, hear, and understand something of what effective communication consists.

"Overheard" conversation can be a valuable means of teaching a person when and how he is:

1. "Beating around the bush" instead of speaking specifically.
2. "Talking off the top of his head" instead of sharing out of his heart.
3. "Reporting" experiences instead of sharing them from his heart.

45

4. Being argumentative, defensive, closed, and guarded instead of open and receptive.

5. Manifesting feelings of sadness, disappointment, anxiety, anger; but not specifically labeling and sharing them.

6. Denying and/or avoiding his feelings.

The degree to which a person learns to show mercy in his relationships is the degree that he will be able to receive mercy. Counseling can be a relationship in which a person learns something of how to receive as well as be merciful towards others.

"BLESSED ARE THE PURE IN HEART FOR THEY WILL SEE GOD."[13]

The basic meaning of the word *pure* is unmixed and unadulterated. The principle under consideration is very demanding of a person. He has to stop, think, and examine himself.[14] A skilled counselor continually looks at himself and his motives for why he is doing what he is with a person. Counseling is looking to see; but Jesus also asked and exhorted:

> Why do you look at the speck of sawdust in your brother's eye and pay no attention to the plank in your own eye? How can you say to your brother, "Let me take the speck out of your eye," when all the time there is a plank in your own eye? You hypocrite, first take the plank out of your own eye, and then you will see clearly to remove the speck from your brother's eye.[15]

It is both a Biblical and psychological fact that it is difficult for a person to understand himself thoroughly and perceive clearly the motives for what he does. Solomon said, "The purposes of a man's heart are deep waters, but a man of understanding draws them out."[16] Jeremiah stated, "The heart is deceitful above all things and beyond cure. Who can understand it."[17] Paul said, "I do not know what I am doing. For what I want to do I do not do, but what I hate I do."[18]

A way of looking at man psychologically is through his conscious and unconscious material. This has been illustrated by the use of a block of ice placed in water. It is clear that by far the larger part of the ice is under the water with the smaller part on top. The smaller part of ice is used to refer to the conscious material with the larger block referring to the unconscious material. Thus, a counselor, without having undergone a great deal of introspection (and that likely with some professional help), has far more reasons for doing what he does in his unconscious mind than he does in his conscious one. Therefore, it becomes very important for a counselor to spend time looking into his reasons for thinking, feeling, and acting the way he does toward himself and others.

STRUCTURE AND CONTRACT ARE NECESSARY FOR EFFECTIVE COUNSELING.

A counselor must counsel out of a solid structure and a clear and precise contract. He does this to facilitate purity in heart of himself and his counselee and to help the client solve his problems.

Structure has reference to the facility in which the counseling takes place as well as the contract negotiated by the counselor and client. The facility should be acceptable to the public and conducive to counseling. The type of setting as well as the type and arrangement of furniture is an important consideration. The facility should communicate a warm and relaxed atmosphere in a professional setting. Ways of accomplishing this are brought out through interior decorating as well as a tape recorder (if used) being visible and other people talking in the building. An important aspect of the structure is the counselor himself, his self-awareness and counseling convictions, which are naturally communicated through his look, posture, tone of voice, and other mannerisms.

The contract is one of the most important aspects of the structure. The counselor should have a clear understanding of his client's expectations of him in counseling. The counselee should have a clear understanding of the counselor's responsibilities in the relationship. Effective counseling necessitates a clear and precise contract between counselor and client. It is the counselor's responsibility to see that the counseling contract is adhered to. It is appropriate to renegotiate a new contract as counseling progresses; but counseling in any area, either at the beginning or later, should not be undertaken without a contract.

Solomon's words of wisdom should be taken seriously by every counselor:

> It is a trap for a man to dedicate something rashly and only later to consider his vows.[19]
>
> Like one who seizes a dog by the ears is a passer-by who meddles in a quarrel not his own.[20]

It is a serious mistake for a person to enter into a relationship without seriously considering his commitment and what it entails. Furthermore, it is a mark of wisdom for an individual not to involve himself in others' problems until invited by them and then only after a sound structure and precise contract has been established.

It is possible for a counselor to enter counseling with mixed and adulterated motives; and likely a counselee will have some impure reasons for beginning counseling, some of which he may not be aware. To the degree, though, that a counselor's motives are unmixed or unadulterated and continue to be so, to that degree he can potentially help a counselee to be pure in heart. The extent to which a counselor's value system is contradictory is commensurate with his impurity of heart. It, therefore, becomes very important for a person who would help another with his impurities to develop an adequate, realistic, and harmonious value system himself.

A COUNSELOR CAN HINDER A CLIENT FROM BECOMING PURE IN HEART.

1. *When he "plays psychiatrist".* The hearts and lives of individuals are sacred and holy. No one has a right after having read a little psychology to "play around" with people as though he were a psychiatrist. A little knowledge is dangerous in the mind and hands of a person unless he accepts that it is a "little". One of the things that disturbs me is the growing number of people who call themselves counselors, but really do not have the credentials.

2. *When he uses his client for a therapist.* It is very easy for the untrained counselor to take advantage of the counselee by using him, what he says and his time, as a means of the counselor's getting things off his chest and sharing his views. Counseling is not a relationship in which a counselor shares his pent-up prejudices and frustrations. Sharing one's personal thoughts, feelings, and experiences should be done discreetly and briefly.

3. *When he attempts to talk a counselee into feeling better through offering him some grandiose promises.* A counselor should never promise a counselee that which he is not sure he can deliver — that the counselee will be feeling better tomorrow and things will be better in his life, marriage, family, etc. A counselor should understand that false hope can make a person emotionally and physically sick, even suicidal. Solomon expressed it this way: "Hope deferred makes the heart sick, but a longing fulfilled is a tree of life."[21]

4. *When he tries to talk his client out of his feelings.* An individual has a right to all of his feelings. Counseling takes those feelings seriously and encourages the individual to become aware of them as well as learn how to express them appropriately, respectfully, and responsibly. This is a mistake frequently made by leaders in the church. Often leaders say such things as, "You should not cry", "You should not feel angry", "You should not be sad". But, notice what Biblical writers have to say:

Rejoice with those who rejoice; mourn with those who mourn.[22]

Like one who takes away a garment on a cold day, or like vinegar poured on soda, is one who sings songs to a heavy heart.[23]

A time to weep and a time to laugh, a time to mourn and a time to dance.[24]

It is better to go to a house of mourning than to go to a house of feasting, for death is in the destiny of every man; the living should take this to heart. Sorrow is better than laughter, because a sad face is good for the heart. The heart of the wise is in the house of mourning, but the heart of fools is in the house of pleasure.[25]

5. *When he merely agrees and/or disagrees with his client.* The underlying issues of which a counselor may be aware, at least to some degree, may be far below the level where a client is speaking. As a rule, there are more issues than those of which the client is aware. A counselor is to raise questions about the underlying problems as well as the presenting ones and not see himself as one who has to agree or disagree with his client.

6. *When he is on a curiosity adventure, witch-hunting, playing detective, or engaging in gossip.* Counseling is not an exercise in which a leader tries to find out the sins of a particular individual or what is "going on" in the church. I know individuals who have been disillusioned seriously with the church and their leaders because, according to them, the leaders inappropriately used what they had shared in counseling.

A counselee should have the right to share his feelings with the counselor about other individuals. However, there is a marked difference between sharing his feelings about another and blaming or accusing him. One effective way a counselor can avoid gossip is by sharing with the counselee something like, "I hear what you are saying, but unless the person is here with us, I see no value in discussing him" or "I would be glad to consider that matter with you and him if you can get him to come for counseling" or "I do not know how to deal with people out of the room, but I am interested in how you are feeling or what is going on in you".

A leader needs to be aware of some basic causes of gossip. An individual gossips because:

a. He does not like something about himself, but likely he will not verbalize it.

b. It is a way of denying and /or avoiding one's own "pain". It can be a way, although ineffective, of trying to deal with one's hurts because a person who gossips has been hurt (not necessarily recently) and is hurting even though he may not be aware of it. It is like, "If I talk about him, − I will feel better − even be healed."

49

c. He is not related to himself and/or to important others in a meaningful and purposeful manner.

d. It may be about the only way a person knows how to vent his feelings. An individual who does not express his emotions in an appropriate manner likely will turn to gossip in order to release some of the pressure which results from a build-up of his feelings.

e. It is a deceptive way of feeling important because gossip does go to and deal with a person's insecurity.

f. He wants to "hurt" someone else.

g. He has been "hurt" and is, therefore, angry. Gossip, though ineffective, is his means of getting his anger out.

7. *When he tries to "figure out" individuals who are not present.* Although it is appropriate to learn theories of human behavior and personality, etc., counseling is not the relationship in which they should be studied directly. This happens to be one of the effective ways people have of subtly moving away from themselves on to someone else. An inexperienced counselor, regardless of his age, likely will fall into this trap.

8. *When he flatters his client.* Paul said, "You know we never used flattery, nor did we put on a mark to cover up greed — God is our witness."[26] Solomon said, "A lying tongue hates those it hurts, and a flattering mouth works ruin."[27]

9. *When he assures his client.* The only blessed assurance that an individual has is honestly accepting Jesus and building his life on His Word. Just as the counselor cannot say that a counselee will feel better and be better tomorrow, he cannot even assure him that counseling will benefit him. Counseling certainly is not for everyone. Even if a person is suited for counseling, it does not mean that he has a guarantee that he will be better by having gone through it. There are a number of determinants, most of which a counselor cannot control, but which affect counseling results.

10. *Where he just talks and laughs.* A counselor or his client could use either talking or laughing to avoid the pain and stress with which they have agreed to deal. In speaking to this matter, Solomon said:

Even in laughter the heart may ache, and joy may end in grief.[28]

The wise in heart accept commands, but a chattering fool comes to ruin.[29]

He who winks maliciously causes grief, and a chattering fool comes to ruin.[30]

A gossip betray a confidence; so avoid a man who talks too much.[31]

A prudent man keeps his knowledge to himself, but the heart of fools blurts out folly.[32]

He who guards his lips guards his soul, but he who speaks rashly will come to

50

ruin.[33]

Even a fool is thought wise if he keeps silent and discerning if he holds his tongue.[34]

11. *When he tries to get the counselee to like him.* An effective counselor does not need a particular counselee to like him. This is not to say that a counselor does not need people to like him — he does. A client has a right to all of his feelings, even his feelings of irritation toward the counselor if they emerge. A counselor needs to be mature enough to respond to his client as Paul did to the Corinthians. For example, he said:

> Even if I caused you sorrow by my letter, I do not regret it. Though I did regret it — to see that my letter hurt you, but only for a little while — yet now I am happy, not because you were made sorry, but because your sorrow led you to repentance. For you became sorrowful as God intended and so were not harmed in any way by us.[35]

12. *When he goes to extremes.* Some of the extremes to be avoided are talking too much or being quiet too long, being too passive or too assertive, being too quick to respond or waiting too long to respond, sounding too righteous, too tender or too tough, being too friendly or too aloof, being too warm or too cold. Solomon said:

> Do not be overrighteous, neither be overwise — why destroy yourself? Do not be overwicked, and do not be a fool — why die before your time? It is good to grasp the one and not let go of the other. The man who fears God will avoid all extremes.[36]

13. *When he relates in a zealous, but not knowledgeable, manner.* Regardless of the depth of one's concern for another and how intense his zeal to help may be, it is not wise to enter a counseling relationship without some insight into oneself and one's motives, knowledge of the counselee and his background, and sound counseling theory.

The following passages speak to this matter in principle:

> It is not good to have zeal without knowledge, nor to be hasty and miss the way.[37]

> Brothers, my heart's desire and prayer to God for the Israelites is that they may be saved. For I can testify about them that they are zealous for God, but their zeal is not based on knowledge. Since they disregarded the righteousness that comes from God and sought to establish their own, they did not submit to God's righteousness.[38]

Sometimes Christian leaders disregard the rigthteousness that comes from God regarding the fundamentals of counseling, which are set forth in His Word, and seek to establish their own theory and methods. In so doing, they limit their effectiveness and increase their potential to do harm. Leaders need to be careful that they not be wise in their own eyes. Hopefully, their concern for helping their followers help themselves would motivate them to do the study necessary to become informed and more effective in their counseling. Solomon said:

Do you see a man wise in his own eyes? There is more hope for a fool than for him.[39]

There is a way that seems right to a man, but in the end it leads to death.[40]

The sluggard is wiser in his own eyes than seven men who answer discreetly.[41]

FOOTNOTES

[1]Matthew 5:7
[2]Barclay,p. 103.
[3]Ibid.
[4]Proverbs 1:10.
[5]1 Corinthians 15:33
[6]2 Thessalonians 5:11.
[7]Hebrews 10:24,25.
[8]2 Corinthians 7:6,7.
[9]Proverbs 22:6.
[10]2 Timothy 1:5.
[11]Proverbs 18:2.
[12]Proverbs 18:13.
[13]Matthew 5:8
[14]Barclay,pp.105,106.
[15]Matthew 7:3-5.
[16]Proverbs 20:5.
[17]Jeremiah 17:9.
[18]Romans 7:15.
[19]Proverbs 20:25.
[20]Proverbs 26:17.
[21]Proverbs 13:12.
[22]Romans 12:15.
[23]Proverbs 25:20.
[24]Ecclesiastes 3:4.
[25]Ecclesiastes 7:2-4.
[26]1 Thessalonians 2:5.
[27]Proverbs 26:28.
[28]Proverbs 14:13.

[29]Proverbs 10:8.
[30]Proverbs 10:10.
[31]Proverbs 20:19.
[32]Proverbs 12:23.
[33]Proverbs 13:3.
[34]Proverbs 17:28.
[35]2 Corinthians 7:8,9.
[36]Ecclesiastes 7:16-18 (Verse 18 footnote A reads:"or will follow them both".
[37]Proverbs 19:2.
[38]Romans 10:1-3.
[39]Proverbs 26:12.
[40]Proverbs 14:12;16:25.
[41]Proverbs 26:16.

Chapter 4

PEACEMAKER OR TROUBLEMAKER?

"Blessed are the peacemakers, for they will be called Sons of God."[1]

Christian counseling is a relationship in which a counselor attempts to help an individual come to peace within himself, with others and God. One of the basic principles in helping individuals solve their problems is for them to be involved with a person who is at peace with himself and who is committed to helping individuals be at peace with themselves. This principle naturally follows the preceding one because it is impossible to be a peacemaker while filled with mixed motives and impurities. There are a number of inappropriate and ineffective interactions in which a counselor and his clients can engage. Such encounters do not produce peace but can contribute to greater conflict and strife.

WAYS OF RELATING WHICH DO NOT LEAD TO PEACE.

1. Since **quarreling and arguing do not lead to peace,** a counselor needs to be alert and exercise caution against getting into an argument with his client. Solomon said:

> Starting a quarrel is like breaching a dam; so drop the matter before a dispute breaks out.[2]
>
> He who loves a quarrel loves sin; he who builds a high gate invites destruction.[3]
>
> It is to a man's honor to avoid strife, but every fool is quick to quarrel.[4]
>
> He who guards his mouth and his tongue keeps himself from calamity.[5]

Paul stated:

> Keep reminding them of these things. Warn them before God against quarreling about words; it is of no value, and only ruins those who listen.[6]
>
> But avoid foolish controversies and genealogies and arguments and quarrels about the law, because these are unprofitable and useless. Warn a divisive person once, and then warn him a second time. After that, have nothing to do with

55

him. You may be sure that such a man is warped and sinful; he is self-condemned.[7]

2. **Telling a person or individuals what they can or cannot do does not make for peace.** I learned years ago that even a teenager is going to do what he wants to do and cannot be "made" to do anything. Obviously, a person can be physically restrained and contained, but I have reference to the fact that a person cannot be "made" to think, feel and be motivated to certain behaviors. This is not to say that a person cannot be influenced or motivated, but my emphasis is on the word **made.** It is quite clear from Scripture that neither God nor Jesus ever tried to make any man do anything. It is just as obvious from a study of the Scriptures that no one in the Godhead ever argued with an individual. God, Christ, and the Holy Spirit gave explicit instructions to an individual by using words from his language and background, and pointed out the consequences of not favorably responding; but Deity was not concerned with "making" an individual do certain things.

3. **Telling a person what to do contributes to discord.** It is presumptous for a counselor to listen to a person for a few minutes and assume that he knows what the individual wants and needs to do. Even if the counselor can establish what an individual needs to do, he should do as Moses, Joshua and the Lord — lay out for the individual the various consequences of different decisions he might make and allow the individual to choose for himself. Notice:

> See, I set before you today life and prosperity, death and destruction. . . .This day I call heaven and earth as witnesses against you that I have set before you life and death, blessings and curses. Now choose life, so that you and your children may live.[8]

> 'But if serving the Lord seems undesirable to you, then choose for yourselves this day whom you will serve, whether the gods your forefathers served beyond the River, or the gods of the Amorites, in whose land you are living. But as for me and my household, we will serve the Lord.'[9]

> 'Come to me, all you who are weary and burdened, and I will give you rest. Take my yoke upon you and learn from me, for I am gentle and humble in heart, and you will find rest for your souls. For my yoke is easy and my burden is light.'[10]

> 'O Jerusalem, Jerusalem, you who kill the prophets and stone those sent to you, how often I have longed to gather your children together, as a hen gathers her chicks under her wings, but you were not willing.'[11]

When a leader listens briefly to an individual (about whom he may know little) share a personal, marital or family problem and feels that he understands him and his problem sufficiently to tell him what he needs, should or can do, he is really being presumptuous.

Due to various reasons, a leader may have little knowledge about an individual, his spouse or family although they may have worshipped together for years. A leader may make the mistake of thinking he knows (has insight into) a person, couple or family because he can call them by name.

A leader who feels he can tell a person what he needs, should and can do, needs to consider seriously:

a. Is he intelligent enough to know this after listening to an individual who likely does not know what he wants and needs himself? Could the person have articulated his problem, need or question with sufficient clarity and precision? A leader may ignore the fact that a person's presenting problem is not usually his core problem. Even if it is, it could have numerous feed roots. Thus, how can he tell him what to do when he has not even heard all of the problem? A leader may ignore the fact that a person shares his thoughts and feelings (if any) as he sees them from his prejudices and not, in reality, as they probably are. I have never known anyone who had such initial perception and depth of insight. There are no precise and simple "ready made" answers to "ready made" questions and problems.

b. Is he perhaps avoiding his own anxiety, guilt, shame, inferior feelings, sense of inadequacy and insecurity? This pattern of thinking and responding to individuals is a way of avoiding one's own feelings and not having to come to grips with them.

c. Does he have the right to take responsibility for another? Paul clearly teaches that an individual is responsible for his own self. He says, "For each man should carry his own load."[12] It is also true that he teaches Christians to "carry each other's burdens."[13] However, there is a vast difference between assisting another and becoming responsible **for** him. A leader has a responsibility **to** and **with** his followers, but he is not responsible **for** them. He has a responsibility to listen and respond to what is being said as well as help a person understand his essential options and the consequences of **his** choices, but he cannot choose for him. Moses, Joshua and Christ emphasized this fact.

Often individuals come to leaders wanting to be told what to do. Perhaps just as often leaders feel they can tell them what to do. A person who has this concept restricts his true leadership ability and effectiveness.

4. **Simply trying to get someone to do, think or feel as the counselor does is inappropriate for a peacemaker.** Although counseling is teaching, it is not actively setting forth one's

beliefs about a certain matter and trying to get the counselee to subscribe to his views. Certainly the counselor should let the client know what his convictions and the make-up of his philosophy are, but this would be done in what is called precounseling and usually takes place in the first session.

5. **Trying to be someone's savior creates more conflict for both counselor and counselee.** If I understand the New Testament, Christ is man's only Savior and, therefore, no one should be attempting to "save" others. It is true that Christians have a responsibility to teach others Christ's philosophy, but that is different from thinking the individual has to save the one being taught. It is easy to brush this point aside, but it is one of the most serious areas to be considered by an individual going into counseling because it is here individuals have some of their greatest disappointments and frustrations. If a leader sincerely desires to be an effective counselor, he must free himself of his "savior complex." Perhaps in counseling as in no other relationship there must be a clear distinction made in the counselor's mind and heart between being a servant and a savior. If this distinction is not made, precisely and clearly, it becomes relatively easy for a counselor to be hurtful in counseling as well as open to quick "burnout". Being a servant, among other things, means that one attempts to give the counselee what he needs and one thing he does not need is the grandiose illusion that the counselor can and will save him.

It is very important for a leader to understand the difference between **helping** someone and **saving** him. While leaders have the responsibility to help, it is not their responsibility to save or **make** someone respond in a particular manner. Granted, their hearts may yearn for a particular response and the desired response may be what the person in reality needs to do, but the choice to respond remains his.

6. **Giving a "lecture" or "sermon" tends to create discord instead of harmony within individuals.** Individuals attend Bible classes and worship services to hear lessons presented and sermons preached. Counseling that is of an intrapersonal and interpersonal nature is not advice-giving. There are academic, legal, and financial counselors who are especially trained to give advice in these matters. An intrapersonal and interpersonal counselor should leave the advice-giving to these people. In fact, this is one of the reasons why a counselor should get the question, "What do you want

58

from me?,," precisely answered early in the first session. If an individual is wanting some advice, then he should be referred to the proper person.

GROWTH IN CHRISTIAN GRACES MAKES FOR PEACE.

One effective way of helping a client to become a peacemaker is through helping him grow in the "Christian graces." Counseling can be a relationship in which a person can learn something of how to increase in faith, goodness, knowledge, self-control, perseverance, godliness, brotherly kindness, and love.[14]

John said, "For everyone born of God has overcome the world. This is the victory that has overcome the world, even our faith."[15] But the **faith** which overcomes the world is not a mere mental assent, but a faith which expresses itself through love. Paul said, "For in Christ Jesus neither circumcision nor uncircumcision has any value. The only thing that counts is faith expressing itself through love."[16] The power of one's faith is rooted in the type of relationships in which he grew up and is currently involved. Paul said, "I have been reminded of your sincere faith, which first lived in your grandmother Lois and in your mother Eunice, and I am persuaded, now lives in you also."[17] He again states, "Therefore, encourage one another and build each other up, just as in fact you are doing."[18]

It is true that the Scriptures can make one wise unto salvation and build him up,[19] but in order for this to be accomplished they must be assimilated into his person, life, and relationships. It is not enough simply to know the Scriptures mentally. The Hebrews writer said, "For we also have had the gospel preached to us, just as they did; but the message they heard was of no value to them, because those who heard did not combine it with faith."[20] It takes time, much effort, and genuine relationships for a person to work through his doubts and develop his trust, to move from memorizing Scriptures to assimilating them; from mental acceptance of Scripture to actually walking by faith. Counseling is a relationship in which these transitions can take place.

Goodness is a quality in which every Christian needs to grow. Christians have a serious problem with really accepting the fact that there is sin in the best of Christians and good in the worst. Many Christians are so "hung up" on either avoiding their sins through arrogance, haughtiness, and sarcasm or just being overwhelmed by their sins. There is not enough genuine effort through lectures, group discussion, sermons, etc., given to helping Christians discover and actualize their goodness. The person who is truly

59

human acknowledges both his worth and his sin. He responds to the grace of God through his faith.

While genuine Christian counseling helps an individual focus specifically on his sin and deal responsibly with it, it also helps him learn how to recognize, accept and cultivate his innate goodness. A Christian counselor is neither afraid of helping a client focus on a sin and deal with it responsibly nor embarrassed in helping a counselee to become aware of "being" good. Once a client sees, accepts, and deals with the sin in his life, a Christian counselor helps him to focus on his goodness.

Christian counseling can be a means of helping a person increase his knowledge. Every Christian certainly is in need of increasing his knowledge of the Bible, self, others, and God and how he should apply the Bible to himself and in his relationships. In regard to the study of Scripture, the word **knowledge** has a much broader context than is often recognized. A person who knows the Scripture will also discover that the Scripture places great emphasis upon who man is and ought to be, morally and religiously.

Each individual Christian needs to increase in self-control. Self-control, though, is not achieved by denying and/or avoiding a part of one's self, especially his heart. Leaders have tended to leave the impression with their followers (whether they were conscious of it or not) that the way to achieve self-control is through repressing and/or suppressing one's emotions. One of the most effective ways of losing control of self is to follow that advice. A person is responsible for his thoughts, feelings, and causes of his behavior and the more accepting he is of himself (thoughts, feelings, behavior) the more likely he can exercise self-control. Counseling can help an individual learn how to be in control of his thoughts, emotions, and behavior.

Perseverance is a quality in which every Christian should increase because it is needed in developing character, rearing responsible children, and cultivating a meaningful marriage. Paul said, "Not only so, but we also rejoice in our sufferings, because we know that suffering produces perseverance; perseverance, character, and character, hope."[21]

Godliness, or becoming like God, is a quality in which each Christian should desire to increase. There is no more effective way for one to become like God than speaking the truth in love, sincerely, specifically, honestly, and with "grace and salt." While looking to see and listening to understand with his own heart, one also increases his godliness as he shares the truth out of his own spirituality. Another way an individual can grow in godliness is by increasing and deepening his fellowship with his fellow Christians and God. One of those fellowship experiences can be counseling.

One quality in which it is difficult for an individual to grow is brotherly kindness. Paul associates compassion and forgiveness with kindness. He said, "Be kind and compassionate to one another, forgiving each other, just as in Christ God forgave you."[22] Kindness implies thoughtful tenderness. Husbands, wives, and children need to learn how to be kind as well as share their kindness.

Two problems many individuals have with their emotions are blocking them out altogether or focusing on one feeling to the exclusion of other feelings. This is often seen with reference to kindness. Although individuals tend to have a problem with appropriately sharing their anger, they tend to have a more difficult problem being able to consistently share genuine kindness.

It is unhealthy for a person to block out his emotions. Awareness and expression (although in an appropriate manner) of an emotion to the exclusion of other emotions is unhealthy also. If all a person does is express anger and not the emotions (disappointment, embarrassment, etc.) which cause his anger then he most definitely becomes an imbalanced individual. Man has a number of emotions and it is to his advantage to learn to recognize, accept and respectfully and responsibly express each of them. To the degree that a person is aware of and appropriately expresses all of his emotions, to that degree he becomes integrated and whole.

Counseling is a relationship in which a person can learn something of how to love himself and live out of a loving frame of reference instead of a fearful one. Therefore, he can learn how to accept and be himself instead of pretending to be who and what he is not. Paul said, "Do everything in love."[23] Counseling, then, is an ongoing relationship in which love is taught to some degree – more nonverbally than verbally, more by what the counselor "is" than by what he "says."

> . . . everyone who loves the father loves his child as well. This is how we know that we love the children of God: by loving God and carrying out his commands. This is love for God: to obey his commands. And his commands are not burdensome.[24]

A person who loves God does what God says, the way He says do it, and for the reason He says do it. A person who loves God will, to the best of his ability, follow His instructions regarding any aspect of his person, life, and relationships. John said:

We love because He first loved us. If anyone says, "I love God," yet hates his brother, is a liar. For anyone who does not love his brother, whom he has seen, cannot love God, whom he has not seen. And he has given us this command: whoever loves God must also love his brother.[25]

It becomes obvious from this passage that how one feels toward his brother and relates to him is a doctrinal matter which must be taken seriously. The Biblical doctrine of love is a doctrine which needs further study and discreet application by religious leaders as well as their followers. This doctrine is far more comprehensive than many leaders and their followers seem to realize.

It is relatively easy for individuals to talk about how they love one another and God, but actually loving one another may be altogether a different matter. John said, "Dear children, let us not love with words or tongue, but with actions and in truth."[26] He also states, "There is no fear in love;"[27] but there are Christians who relate to each other more out of fear, shame, or guilt than from love. Couples have shared that they have remained married, not out of genuine love for one another, but more out of the shame they would feel if the brethren knew they had problems. It is easy to talk about loving, but the sad reality is that in some marriages, families, and congregations individuals treat each other with less respect than they do their pets.

Perhaps no factor is as important in the understanding of human nature as the concept of love. The greatest of all needs of a person is the need of love. It is just as important for a person to **give** love as it is for him to **receive** it.

Since love is taught and not inherited, it must be learned in situations where love is expressed, because without love — love cannot grow. From an infant on, one needs to receive love unconditionally, consistently and dependably. Although a child needs to learn tenderness and affection, he should not be overly-hugged, kissed and petted. There should not be unpredictable shifts, as there are in some families, between ardent affection one moment and strong rejection the next. Furthermore, parents should love their children because of "who they are" and not "what they do."

One learns to love in a home where one is free to express affections spontaneously without fear or rebuke, in relation to companions who share positive, emotional responses mutually. But, authentic love received in a dependable relationship is based upon the type parents a person had. If his parents were taught to love themselves, they can love their children.

If this basic need is not fulfilled, an infant may die; or if he manages to survive, he will probably be cold, selfish, egotistical, aggressive or jealous. Inasmuch as some have never experienced genuine love, they are confused and have intense craving for superiority, power, wealth, cleverness, success, independence, glamour and pride; not understanding that what their children really want and need is mother, father and their unconditional love.

Since one's need to give and receive love does not cease with age, one of the goals of counseling with a particular client may be to help him learn how to meet his need for love. Naturally, to achieve this goal may require considerable time and much effort.

FOOTNOTES

[1]Matthew 5:9.
[2]Proverbs 17:14.
[3]Proverbs 17:19.
[4]Proverbs 20:3.
[5]Proverbs 21:23.
[6]2 Timothy 2:14.
[7]Titus 3:9-11.
[8]Deuteronomy 30:15,19.
[9]Joshua 24:15.
[10]Matthew 11:28-30.
[11]Matthew 23:37.
[12]Galatians 6:5.
[13]Galatians 6:2.
[14]2 Peter 1:5-9.
[15]1 John 5:4.
[16]Galatians 5:6.
[17]2 Timothy 1:5.
[18]1 Thessalonians 5:11.
[19]2 Timothy 3:15; Acts 20:32.
[20]Hebrews 4:2.
[21]Romans 5:3-4.
[22]Ephesians 4:32.
[23]1 Corinthians 16:14.
[24]1 John 5:1-3.

[25] 1 John 4:19-21.
[26] 1 John 3:18.
[27] 1 John 4:18.

Chapter 5

DECISION MAKING – A PERSONAL RESPONSIBILITY

"BLESSED ARE THOSE WHO ARE PERSECUTED BECAUSE OF RIGHTEOUSNESS FOR THEIRS IS THE KINGDOM OF HEAVEN."[1]

MAKING DECISIONS IS DIFFICULT

One of the most difficult things for a person to do when in a crisis or faced with a problem in general is to thoroughly analyze it and make **his** decision in light of both short and long range consequences. Although an individual needs the approval of others, there are decisions which he alone must make.

A person needs to realize that people have impressions of him regardless of the type of decisions he makes. Some will agree and others will disagree; therefore, "opinion polls" should not be the bases on which a person makes his decision. "Opinion polls" are like the wind; they shift and change sometimes swiftly and radically.

When a person is making a decision, he should consider what others may think, but keep in mind what Jesus and Peter said:

> Woe to you when all men speak well of you, for that is how their fathers treated the false prophets.[2]

> If you suffer, it should not be as a murderer or thief or any kind of criminal, or even as a meddler. However, if you suffer as a Christian, do not be ashamed, but praise God that you bear that name.[3]

REMEMBER YOUR ROOTS

One mistake made by religious leaders is that they tend to encourage people to "forget" or "not think about," and thus not remember, experiences in the past. Probably every leader would encourage people to remember pleasant, joyous, and meaningful experiences of the past, but many feel that there is no value in recalling painful experiences in one's life. No one has the right to inflict pain on another, but a person has a right and should experience his pain in its season. Otherwise, it will linger, likely get worse, and become more controlling of a person. Of course, such recall is unhealthy if one gets "stuck" with a painful memory and retreats from life and its responsibilities. However, remembering one's pain and sharing it in an open, honest, respectful, and responsible relationship, which is properly and adequately structured, can be healthy and spiritually productive.

Memory, which is immediately available to a person, can be a powerful, stabilizing force in his life if somehow it becomes a way of discovering something of the meaning of the experience. A person's pain (disappointment, shame, guilt, anxiety, grief, etc.), when accepted, understood, shared, confessed or worked through (verbally and nonverbally) by him, can be an effective means of discovering something of the meaning and purpose of his life.

Christian leaders need to be seriously concerned about and effectively involved with their followers in helping them to discover and digest the meaning of their thoughts, feelings, and behaviors. Emphasis is often placed on the plan of salvation, the nature and organization of the church, and worship (and this is needed), but oftentimes little emphasis of an analytical and detailed nature is given to helping individuals discover the meaning of what they are doing. It would be a mark of wisdom for leaders to take Moses seriously when he said regarding the Passover, "And when your children ask you, 'What does this ceremony mean to you?' then tell them, 'It is the passover sacrifice to the Lord, who passed over the houses of the Israelites in Egypt and spared our homes when he struck down the Egyptians.' "[4]

Peter emphasized memory. Regarding the Christian graces, he said that a person who did not increase in those qualities would become ineffective and unproductive in his knowledge of Christ.[5] Then he stated, "But if anyone does not have them, he is nearsighted and blind, and has forgotten that he has been cleansed from his past sins."[6] He then continues:

So I will always remind you of these things, even though you know them and are firmly established in the truth you now have. I think it is right to refresh your memory as long as I live in the tent of this body, because I know that I will soon put it aside, as our Lord Jesus Christ made clear to me. And I will make every effort to see that after my departure you will always be made to remember these things.[7]

The above passages clearly show that a person who does not increase in the "Christian graces" is one who not only becomes nearsighted and blind, but forgets that he has been cleansed from his sins. Therefore, there are certain things that a person needs to remember in order to continue to grow as a Christian. It is, therefore, to one's advantage to remember how he came to be the way he is, and an effective means of remembering whence he came is a continual growing in the qualities which Peter set forth.

A counselor can help a client remember through such responses as:

1. Does that remind you of anything else in your life?
2. Does she or he remind you of anyone else?
3. You look sad today. Do you know what is causing your sadness?
4. Did you ever feel like this as a young child?
5. I wonder what it was like for you growing up?
6. What pleasant memories of growing up do you recall?
7. What unpleasant memories do you have?
8. Were you ever sad and lonely?
9. Can you recall having feelings like these before?

A person thinks, feels, and acts toward himself and others largely because of the environment in which he was reared. The more an individual has repressed and/or suppressed the influences of his earlier environment the more likely he is controlled by them. Counseling, therefore, can be a relationship in which a person can regress through memory, relive with insight, and through confession or sharing (verbally and nonverbally) work through those earlier influences so that he is no longer controlled by them although he continues to be influenced by them.

An individual who was overprotected and not taught how to think through the components of a problem will have difficulty making his decisions and accepting the consequences. He may want his spouse, employer, religious leader, or counselor to tell him what to do. It is easy for a counselor when approached by this type of person to think that helping him consists of thinking for and telling him what to do. The longer this type of individual gets people to try and be "responsible for him," the more frustrated and the less rewarding his life will become. A skilled counselor perceives counseling as a relationship in which an individual is helped (not told) in understanding the process of how to make an effective decision as well as being supported by some other concerned individual during the time he is learning.

One of the reasons why a person does not want to make his decisions is he would be faced with the consequences of them. Part of the consequences may be the disagreement or "persecution" he would receive from others. But the person who grew up making "his decisions" (which grew out of truth or righteousness), accepting the consequences, and learning from them discovered he was "blessed" or "fortunate" even though he may have been persecuted at the time.

A CLIENT NEEDS TO MAKE "HIS" DECISIONS

An effective counselor does not tell another person what to do. In fact, one function of counseling is helping a client to understand that he is responsible for his own thoughts, feelings, and actions. In addition, the counselee needs to understand that counseling is his choice and **he is responsible for what** is dealt with in the relationship. One mistake some counselors make is thinking they are responsible for the agenda of the hour. However, it is the counselor's responsiblity to set appropriate structure, work out an effective contract, and be available to his client (intellectually and emotionally) as he discovers and works through his problem.

The process of making an informed personal decision is complicated and can be very frustrating and painful. Many individuals do not know how to creatively confront their frustration and likely believe that their pain cannot be valuable for them. They tend to avoid their frustration and pain by "jumping into" a decision quickly and with little thought.

Every decision a person makes has some advantages and disadvantages with both short and long-range consequences. It is to one's advantage to understand as thoroughly as possible what each of these are before he decides, not after.

There are emergency decisions which need immediate attention; but as a rule, a person has ample time in which to make most of his decisions. An individual should not be in the habit of rushing into deciding. A person needs time to think through the components of a decision and allow his ambivalent feelings to emerge. Once they are surfaced, he needs time to process his ambivalence.

COMPONENTS OF A DECISION

There are certain components of a decision which need to be considered:

1. Most likely there are unconscious reasons why a person will make a particular choice. Most people will probably have as many, if not more, unconscious reasons for making a decision as conscious ones. The more personal, comprehensive, and important the decision (for example, getting married, having children, deciding one's vocation), the more likely there will be unconscious reasons for deciding.

2. A person makes decisions much the same way he was trained by his parents or other significant individuals. The degree of understanding a person has about his past is proportionate to his awareness of how his parents trained him to make decisions. On the surface, a child may think he is not like his parents; but the clearer his perception of what is underneath, the clearer he can see how much like his parents he really is. If his parents lived impulsively and not intentionally, he will likely do the same unless he has recognized, accepted, and worked through those dynamics within him.

3. When making a decision, a person attempts to meet a particular need(s). The more personal the decision, the more likely he can be confused about the need(s) and how to meet it satisfactorily. An individual who needs affection may have illicit sex as a means of trying to get it. A person who needs to experience his sadness may get drunk to avoid it. An individual may need to be complimented or get the approval of another, but tries to meet it through being hypercritical and sarcastic. A person may need security (love), but becomes jealous and envious.

4. A person usually thinks he is making a decision in his best interest, but he may be looking at the immediate and not the long-range consequences. He may be caught up in his anxiety and not face the consequential reality. He may be wanting only sympathy and agreement, but verbalize that he wants what is best, appropriate, or right.

Effective Decisions Grow Out of Ambivalence

I am convinced that effective decision making grows out of one's ambivalence being recognized, accepted and worked through prior to when the decision is made. Ambivalence is simply the emerging of negative and positive feelings toward the immediate as well as the distant possible consequences of the decision.

It should be understood that every decision has both its short-range and long-range consequences — advantages and disadvantages. This being true, the time to experience frustration, anxiety, doubt, questions, anger, etc. is before a person makes a particular decision, not afterwards.

If ambivalence is not recognized, accepted and worked through before a decision is made, it will emerge afterwards. Serious problems may occur as a result. A person may feel panicky, anxious, trapped, and resentful. Even though the consequences are inevitable, a person may choose not to face them squarely and deal with them responsibly.

One way of helping a client make his decision is to raise as much unconscious material into his conscious as possible, and then help him to look at it as critically and as analytically as possible before he decides. One reason for doing this is that most of the reasons why a person does or does not make a particular decision (especially if it is very important to him) may be in his unconcious mind. Therefore, a skilled counselor, understanding this, helps raise this material through appropriate questions and suggestions into the client's conscious mind so he has it available to him for considering.

PERSONAL DECISIONS MAKE FOR MATURITY

The beatitudes describe the truly whole or integrated individual. It should be understood that maturity is relative; it is a process and not a fixed fact or state. How a person makes and follows through on decisions indicate his level of maturity or integration.

Self-knowledge or insight, acceptance and personal responsibility are prerequisites to maturity. One should examine himself, with the view in mind of ascertaining why he feels, thinks, and acts the way he does. In fact, the achievement of insight is necessary if he becomes free and mature. However, genuine self-understanding is of no practical value unless one accepts himself, not as he wishes he were nor as others say he is, but as he in reality is. One cannot change himself until he accepts himself as he actually is. But acceptance of one's self (as important as this is) does not solve one's problems. An individual's problems will never be solved unless he accepts himself, but the moment of acceptance is not that of solution. At this point a person still has the change to make – he must assume personal responsibility – taking realistic and adequate action. Obviously, acceptance is neither changing nor solving the problem, although it is a requisite to its solution.

When a person sees himself as he is, accepts his real self, and takes corrective and constructive steps, he can develop into a mature, effectively functioning individual. He, therefore, can really accept the fact that to be human is to err. One of man's fundamental needs is that of honestly looking introspectively although few people seem to effectively practice it. Nevertheless, one of the basic prerequisites of a mature person is the courage to deny himself the luxury of alibis.

70

Every informed individual knows that personal deception is possible, and in order to avoid this disturbing recognition of the genuine self, some resort to rationalization. This is not new because Jesus dealt with other's rationalization:

> But they all alike began to make excuses. The first said, 'I have just bought a field, and I must go and see it. Please excuse me.' Another said, 'I have just bought five yoke of oxen, and I'm on my way to try them out. Please excuse me.' Still another said, 'I just got married, so I can't come.'¹

Rationalization is self-deception and the capacity which a person has for it is enormous. The mind has almost limitless powers to deceive oneself. Rationalization is a device of respectability by which one protects and pampers himself and in some situations, (such as a serious accident or death of a loved one) up to a point, is healthy. This is its primary function. The aim is to be acceptable because it deals with appearances rather than realities; what looks good instead of what is true. The reasoning used is designed not to discover or defend what may be true. It is a preference for good reasons instead of real ones, to explain what one has done or failed to do, being the colored glasses through which he looks at reality. It is finding reasons to justify an act after it has been performed or a decision after it has been made. Rationalizing is a process of justifying oneself, his beliefs, peers, and group. One of the most common uses of rationalization is that of a person denying that he practices it.

An integrated individual can resist stress and has a unifying outlook on life. He has the ability to see life clearly — as it is, not as he wishes it to be. He does not allow his hopes and wishes to distort his observations. Because of his superior perception, he is more decisive and has a clearer understanding of what is right and wrong. He is able to make his own decisions even in the face of contrary popular opinions.

A mature person knows that no one is exempt from misunderstanding and misrepresentation. It is clear to him that some criticism is just and constructive. On the other hand, some is made unjustly, the motive being to hurt him and/or destroy his influence. He is keenly conscious that some misrepresent him by not telling all of the truth, none of it, or part of the truth mixed with falsehood. Also, one may by voice inflection and emotion convey the wrong impression, but the result is the same.

In dealing with criticism and using it to one's advantage, one must wisely appraise it before accepting or rejecting it. The mature individual knows that it is possible for a person to learn valuable truths about himself from his critics. Adversity can be of more value than prosperity. It is a true adage that any person should beware when all men speak well of him. However, an integrated person makes a fetish neither of conformity nor of nonconformity, but guards his own integrity and freedom of judgment.

Self-discipline is relatively easy because what he desires to do agrees with what he believes is right. When he does so he genuinely admits or confesses it. Accepting the fact that he and all men sin, but that forgiveness is possible, puts him in a frame of mind which is more conducive to friendliness towards himself and others. Much unfriendliness towards others has its taproot in a dislike of and unfriendliness toward self. This is partly true because one does not see himself as in reality he is, and/or refuses to accept himself as he is, and/or does not know or rejects the necessary corrective and development steps.

An integrated person is less afraid of himself and his environment. He is not like the one talent man who said: "I knew that you are a hard man, harvesting where you have not sown and gathering where you have not scattered seed. So I was afraid and went out and hid your talent in the ground. See, here is what belongs to you."[9]

An integrated individual is creative and flexible – able to change as the situation changes, to break habits, to face indecision and changes in conditions without undue stress. He is not threatened by the unexpected as rigid, unflexible people. He is in control of himself and his destiny (this does not mean that he does not trust in God and walk by faith in Him); not ashamed of himself, or discouraged by his mistakes. He has a kind of humility which enables him to listen carefully to others, to admit that he does not know everything and that others can teach him something. He is adapted to his environment displaying a creative capacity for love, work, and play. He maintains a stable set of internal standards for his actions, so that he is relatively independent of social influences.

The more an individual is given to making his own decisions and accepting the inevitable consequences of such decisions, the happier and healthier he becomes. The person who truly approaches life through the principles set forth in the beatitudes becomes the "salt of the earth" and the "light of the world." Counseling can be a means of helping a person grow in this process.

TRUTH WITHOUT SELLOUT

A person who solves his problems is one who buys the truth and does not sell it.[10] Although truth frees,[11] cleanses,[12] and purifies;[13] it may be difficult to discover and assimilate in a given situation. It is important for one to perceive clearly that his thoughts, opinions, and prejudices may neither be the truth nor related to it in a given case. In addition, once an individual has discovered truth, there may very well be strong temptations to sell it or compromise when trying to solve a particular problem. Clear distinction should be made between compromising one's opinions, ideas, traditions and biases from compromising a principle on truth. Solomon said, "Buy the truth and do not sell it. Get wisdom, discipline and understanding."[14]

FOOTNOTES

[1]Matthew 5:10.
[2]Luke 7:26.
[3]1 Peter 4:15,16.
[4]Exodus 12:26,27.
[5]2 Peter 1:8.
[6]2 Peter 1:9.
[7]2 Peter 1:12-15.
[8]Luke 14:18-20.
[9]Matthew 25:24,25.
[10]Proverbs 23:23.
[11]John 8:32.
[12]John 15:3.
[13]1 Peter 1:22.
[14]Proverbs 23:23.

Chapter 6

REASONS WHY PEOPLE COME FOR COUNSELING

WHAT DO YOU KNOW ABOUT YOUR CLIENT?

A leader needs specific information about the individual, couple or family who is wanting to be involved in counseling with him. Many times a local leader will have some knowledge of his client before he comes for counseling, but this is not always the case. Even when it is, there needs to be time spent in obtaining more history before beginning counseling.

The family history should include such things as:

1. What his parents were like; their ages, how they related and/or did not relate to each other and the children, their occupations, education and where they were reared.

2. If client had siblings, where in the family was he born.

3. Any traumatic experiences in his life such as deaths, moves, divorce, separation and disappointments and at what age these occurred.

4. What educational, social, religious and sexual histories are involved.

5. What support systems are available to him in terms of extended family and friends as well as what use, if any, he makes of these.

6. How he would answer the three questions: What do you want from me? Why did you come to see me? Why did you come now? (These answers are very important to the understanding of one's client.)

PSYCHOLOGY, A FRIEND – NOT AN ENEMY

Some psychological testing would help a leader to know something about whether he is skilled enough to be of help to a particular counselee. Of course, if he discovers that he is not, an appropriate referral would be in order.

A person cannot expect to do satisfactory work without a knowledge of human behavior. Actually, a counselor must understand the growth, dynamics, and problems of personality in order to be skillful. Psychology can be effective in giving an individual clearer insight into how people think, feel, and why they behave as they do. It is not only a possible authentic auxiliary for aiding others, but as one understands and helps others, he can be learning about his own thoughts and feelings and why he acts as he does.

Since a number of the theories on the nature of man were developed by naturalistic psychologists, it is only natural that these theories would leave out the spiritual dimension of man altogether or treat it differently from the way the Bible does. The number of psychiatrists and psychologists who believe in God may not be as great as those who do not believe in Him, but there are many psychiatrists and psychologists who recognize and even emphasize the spiritual dimension of man. The fact that there are extremists in both psychologists and religion does not rule out legitimate, therapeutic, and constuctive application of both to the human personality. Psychology can be an outstanding auxiliary to a counselor, but the psychological soundness of the Bible does not harmonize with everything in psychology. This should not be alarming, though, because positions have been abandoned and variations between schools of thought do exist.

In addition to specific information about a client, a leader needs general knowledge about why individuals come for counseling.

UNRESOLVED CONFLICTS

Couples of families usually come because they have not solved the *little conflicts* which have erupted in their relationship through the years. Since these conflicts produced minor irritations and disappointments within the individuals, they most likely concluded that they were too minor to deserve serious attention. They may have tried to *forget* or *ignore* them. A leader needs to understand that, as a rule, individuals do not have serious and prolonged major problems. They usually have a number of minor problems which have accumulated over the years. After having been repeated many times and never really resolved, these problems have become knotted up in such a fashion that it is very difficult for the individuals with the problems to separate and see them for what they are.

PRESENTING PROBLEM IS NOT THE ROOT

The *official* or presenting problem is not always the root problem. However, the *official* problem should be heard by the counselor and not dismissed too quickly or the individual(s) may feel the counselor has rejected him. If the presenting problem is dismissed too soon, an individual may feel that he and his problem are not important and are not being taken seriously by the counselor. How the counselee feels the counselor has dealt with his *official* problem has a great deal to do with whether counseling will continue and, to some degree, how effective it will be if continued.

A person neither thoroughly understands what his problem is nor clearly perceives how it relates to other aspects of himself, his relationships and his life. Sometimes this lack of perception and differentiation is obvious to a counselor. An individual who is logical and/or articulate can be deceptive; therefore, a wise counselor listens with discernment.

CLIENT MAY TALK AROUND HIS EMOTIONS INSTEAD OF SHARING THEM

An individual is more likely to talk around his emotions than he is to share them. He is more likely to describe and explain his behavior, give reasons for why he did or did not do what he did, and tell what or how he thinks than he is to share his feelings.

A person is more likely to speak ambiguously, even in the second and third persons, than he is to talk straight or be precise when expressing himself.

An individual is more likely to blame others for his problems (sometimes the blaming is very subtle) than he is to own them and take responsibility for himself in solving them.

A person who is sad, depressed and hurting is more likely to feel sorry for himself and want somebody to take care of him than he is to experience his pain genuinely and work through it. *A counselor needs to be aware that there is a fine line between experiencing and working through one's pain and feeling sorry for one's self, wallowing in one's pity and wanting another to take his pain away.* It is helpful for a person to experience his pain, but it is easy for him to cease experiencing it and begin wallowing in his self–pity. Often it takes a counselor with trained eyes, ears and heart to distinguish between an individual's experiencing his pain and feeling sorry for himself and wanting another to take care of him; that is, solve his problem or do his hurting for him.

Things are not necessarily the way the client says they are. He may be intentionally deceiving or, at best, giving his distorted or colored perception of how he sees them. He may be so confused that he is not even aware of this distortion.

WHAT OR WHO DOES CLIENT WANT CHANGE?

An individual may be of the opinion that change is brought about through a counselor's sharing intellectual ideas or concepts. Teaching of this nature may be of some value and even needed in some cases, but a counselor is limiting his ability to help when he is not prepared to aid people in digesting and assimilating concepts into the way they think, feel and behave. Most people who come to a counselor do not need new information, but someone who will help them learn how to resolve the conflicts and work through the pain they are currently experiencing. Through such learning they hopefully become more effective in relating with one another and managing their conflicts.

A person usually comes saying that he wants to change and sometimes he can be rather specific as to what he wants changed. He does not likely realize that, while he says he wants to change, at the same time he will struggle not to change. A counselor needs to recognize and understand this dynamic or else he may end up focusing on the individual in a negative way rather than analyzing the resistance. It sounds pleasant and comfortable for one to say he wants to change, but for change really to take place there must be persistent struggling with the individual's pain, etc. A counselor needs to realize that an individual must be allowed to change at his own pace. Otherwise, the counselor may be only frustrating the individual and really interfering with the change process.

A counselor needs to help the counselee specifically identify what it is that he is wanting to change. Unless this is clearly defined, a counselor may find himself trying to get the counselee to change something in which he is not really interested in changing. It is important for a counselor to get specific answers to the following questions: What do you want from me? Why did you come to me instead of someone else? Why did you come to me now? It is also important for a counselor to help the counselee clarify what he wishes to change. Does the counselee feel that the counselor can bring about the change with little or no involvement in the process on his part? Is the counselee interested in changing some behavior, some intellectual concept or academic matter, a particular attitude, a particular feeling or a combination of these. These points need to be clearly delineated, especially in the counselor's mind or a counselor and counselee may become lost in their confusion and exasperated in their efforts.

A counselor needs a clear and precise definition of what he means by change. Does it mean eradication, modification, adjustment, acceptance, fuller awareness, more freedom of expression or being and experiencing oneself? Behavior can be modified, adjusted or eliminated, but can one eliminate his basic emotions? A person can modify, adjust, suppress or repress, but can he really eliminate a basic emotion? It is necessary for the serious student of change to clearly understand what one means by change, as well as to what extent change takes place and how transient or permanent it is. Change is a process which may modify, adjust or even eliminate certain behaviors. It is important to remember that behavior is symptomatic and not the root problem.

A counselor or counselee may feel that changing one's environment changes his person. It is true that environment influences a person, but one is not changed simply by altering his behavior or improving his environment. For example, it is probable that an alcoholic will not change his behavior (quit his drinking) while in an alcoholic environment. One should not assume, however, that just because an alcoholic changes his environment, he will be a changed person. Although change may include altering one's environment, behavior, and how one feels about his basic emotions, it is incorrect to think that an individual can substitute one for the other. For example, in dealing with one's grief, a person needs to return to his regular responsibilities; but assuming his responsibilities will not substitute for the need to experience his pain through weeping – it takes both.

New or different behavior may create in a person new or different feelings, but behavior cannot change the feelings he already has unless that behavior is an expression of those feelings and/or directly related to them. An individual cannot change a basic feeling (in the sense of eliminating it - sexual, need for affection, belonging, self-esteem or worth). He can change (even eliminate) *how* he feels about his feelings or emotions and his behavior which is an expression of those feelings and/or directly related to them.

Jesus stated that the real issues are in the heart. Although a person does not change (eliminate) his basic emotions (heart), he can emotionally regress and bring into consciousness the pain, disappointment, shame or guilt (real/unreal) from the past. Although how he was formed and/or deformed by relationships in the past still influences him, he can work through these feelings to the point that he is not controlled or absolutely determined by the past, but is freed up to make clearer choices in the present.

PAIN AND A DESIRE TO BE CONFLICT FREE MOTIVATES ONE TO SEEK COUNSELING

Likely everyone who comes for counseling has pain. An individual, couple or family may be unaware of their pain or cannot articulate it. Nevertheless, they are hurting. A counselor should be concerned about getting as clearly focused on the pain as possible during the first session. One of the ways of doing this is simply raising questions like:

"Where are you hurting?"
"What is causing your pain?"
"Are you aware of your pain and what is causing it?"
"I sense your pain. Will you share it with me?"
"You are in pain. I wonder if you would share it with me?"

In many cases a counselor's effectiveness will be determined to a great degree on how effective he is in getting the client to focus on and share his pain. Since pain stirs up pain, a counselor must be comfortable with and to a great degree have accepted and worked through his own pain. Otherwise, he will not allow the client to work through his pain.

Clients most likely feel they should be conflict free. One goal of the counselor should be to help clients resolve and manage their conflict rather than try to live without conflict. Conflict is a part of living and it is important that an individual learn how to manage his conflict. One effective way individuals have of increasing their tension, as well as their conflicts, is to sincerely believe and try to operate or live in a way in which there would be no conflict. Since conflict is inevitable, a person may spend all of his time and energies trying to figure out a way to live conflict free instead of learning how to manage or solve conflicts when they do arise.

Couples and families come because of the pain that grows out of trying to live in fantasy or an ideal rather than with reality. So often in sermons and lessons the ideal is presented as though it were reality. Individuals tend to fantasize and pretend things are not the way they are. Fantasy, dreaming or planning is appropriate so long as an individual separates his fantasies from reality, lives in the real world and builds his plans and hopes out of reality. Every individual creates his fantasies to avoid reality. Temporary avoidance is healthy so long as the individual knows he is avoiding and does so only temporarily. A serious danger develops when an individual gets so confused that his fantasies become reality to him.

DISAPPOINTMENT CAUSES INDIVIDUALS TO COME FOR COUNSELING

Usually when a person comes to a counselor, he is disappointed. This is certainly true of couples and families. Marriage and family have been a disappointment to him. It did not turn out as he had dreamed and planned. His marriage was built on fantasy, romanticism or some other unreal concept and not on realistic hope. Hope which is made of substance and not "wishful thinking" does not disappoint one. Paul said, "We also rejoice in our sufferings, because we know that suffering produces perseverance; perseverance, character; and character, hope. And hope does not disappoint us."[1] The Hebrews writer stated, "Now faith is being sure of what we hope for and certain of what we do not see."[2] Again the Hebrews writer stated, "We who have fled to take hold of the hope offered to us may be greatly encouraged. We have this hope as an anchor for the soul, firm and secure."[3] Again Paul said, "For in this hope we were saved. But hope that is seen is no hope at all. Who hopes for what he already has? But if we hope for what we do not yet have, we wait for it patiently."[4]

The wise man stated:

> The prospect of the righteous is joy, but the hopes of the wicked come to nothing.[5]
> When a wicked man dies, his hope perishes; all he expected from his power comes to nothing.[6]
> Hope deferred makes the heart sick, but a longing fulfilled is a tree of life.[7]
> A longing fulfilled is sweet to the soul, but fools detest turning from evil.[8]

FIX MY SPOUSE AND EVERYTHING WILL BE OKAY

Couples who come for counseling do so with the belief that if his partner would change, the marriage would be much better. Each is hoping the counselor will "fix" his spouse. This is most likely true even if one spouse is, at least verbally, taking responsibility for the problems in the marriage. Almost every family has a problem child or "patient" and, when coming to counseling, the family assumes that the "patient" will be treated and the family will be healed. Most of the time families are not aware that a particular member is picked

81

for the "patient" as a means of escaping problems with other family members which may be more difficult and threatening to deal with.

LET'S FIGURE OUT MY SPOUSE

An individual may want to spend his time getting the counselor to figure out what is wrong with his spouse, child or someone else. If a counselor falls for this "subtle trap," he will in reality not be counseling. This is not to say that a counselor and client may not contract for pre-counseling sessions in which he may do some teaching. However, even in this type of contractual situation, he should not get involved in the "trap" of trying to figure out why a particular husband or child behaves as he does.

I AM INNOCENT

When there is a sexual affair in a marriage, most often the so-called innocent one has also been having an affair. A spouse can have an affair with his job, children, education, hobby, reading, watching television, etc. A person is having an affair when he emotionally and/or physically withdraws from his spouse and seeks to get his needs met through concentrating his emotional and physical energies in whoever or whatever becomes the substitute for his spouse. In this context, having an affair is being unfaithful to one's commitments.

I AM LOOKING FOR A QUICK CURE

An individual, couple or family may come looking for a miracle or some magical response from the counselor which will make everything right. One potential problem of a counselor is to feel that he does have magic, can work miracles and solve all problems. A counselor needs to understand not only does he not have any *tricks,* but there are no *tricks* to be found. There are principles to be discovered, understood and utilized, but there is no magic.

TELL ME WHAT TO DO AND I WILL PROVE YOU WRONG

Individuals usually come to the counselor to be told what to do. Underneath, they may just be wanting someone to agree that where they are and what they are doing are acceptable. If any change needs to be made, they feel it should be the other person. They may be wanting to prove their problem is unsolvable, etc., so they ask for information and then go out and prove the counselor was wrong.

A couple may be wanting an excuse to say they have been for counseling and it has not helped so they can continue as they are doing or end the marriage.

PERSONS COME OUT OF RESPECT FOR ONE'S AUTHORITY

Individuals come to a Christian leader because of his authority and their respect for what he represents. The reverse of this is also true. Every leader needs to understand that "God did not give us a spirit of timidity, but a spirit of power, of love and self-discipline."[9]

WATCH OUT FOR SEDUCTION

A counselor needs to accept the fact that people coming for counseling are sometimes seductive. A counselor may make some costly mistakes if he does not understand, accept and is comfortable with his own sexuality. In addition, he needs to be a person who is sensitive to seductive clues that take place in all types of relationships. The various clues fall into such areas as touch, use of one's eyes, posture, gestures, body, and words associated with nonverbal communication. A skilled counselor is aware of seduction taking place on both a conscious and unconscious level. He also understands that he must not only listen to what a person is saying or not saying, but with his therapist's ear catch and distinquish the subtle changes in an individual's voice, speech rate, gestures, etc., which give clues to underlying meanings to otherwise innocent remarks.

A word of caution is in order at this point. A novice counselor may pick up a book or two on body language and try to make something out of everything he sees or hears. A skilled counselor notices the shifts, patterns, verbal and nonverbal contradictions and does not form an opinion simply by hearing or seeing a particular technique he has read from a book. Nevertheless, a skilled counselor does understand that "as water reflects a face, so a man's heart reflects the man."[10]

The seductive process is clearly set forth by Solomon. Even though he makes reference to woman as being seductive, the principles would apply to man. It can be established (from Scripture and clinical material) that sexual seduction is an impersonal (physical) attempt at meeting a personal need (such as self-worth, affection, etc.). It is used by an individual to say (though he may be confused and deceptive), "I need to know if you like me." "I need you to notice me." It is a way a person has of trying to determine if he is *truly loveable* or *somebody*. Solomon said, "Like a gold ring in a pig's snout is a beautiful woman who shows no discretion."[11]

It seems obvious that a counselor needs to have a clear understanding and acceptance of his own sexuality and his motives for counseling with a particular person. Furthermore, he needs to understand that he has *blind spots* and protect himself by setting appropriate structure, getting a clearly defined contract. It is wise to have a skilled consultant before beginning counseling as well as during the process.

It should be understood that seduction can and does take place in various relationships and at different levels – not just in counseling. A wise counselor grows in understanding himself, his needs and how to meet them appropriately and responsibly, as well as in his perception of the seductive process and how to respond to it effectively – neither avoiding nor denying it.

COUPLES AND FAMILIES HAVE NUMEROUS CONTRACTS

Couples and families come for counseling with numerous conscious and unconscious contracts which may add to or create additional conflicts in the marriage or family. These contracts can be individual, couple or group. For example, a husband may contract with himself to never talk about a particular problem with his wife. So often these contracts relate to how he feels about himself, sex, religion and finances. A couple may agree verbally and/or nonverbally not to mention a certain matter with the counselor. The children may agree to not mention dad's sexual advances.

Many contracts are nonverbally made with a certain look or glance, tone of voice, gesture, etc., but are powerfully binding. Contracts which are made early in relationships are often forgotten but are still forcefully in effect. Contracts are often made out of one's own prejudices, contradictory values in how he sees himself in different roles (husband, father, etc.) and how a marriage and family "ought to function."

The more verbal ambiguity and/or the more unconscious the inherent components of a contract are, likely the more conflict there will be trying to enforce it and will possibly be met with greater resistance. Ambiguous and unconscious contracts are difficult to recognize and accept as well as enforce to each one's satisfaction.

Contracts are agreements which an individual has with himself, his spouse or other family members. The agreement may be practiced or binding not because of consent, but because of uncontrollable forces such as guilt, shame or fear. Contracts may continue in force because the parties just do not understand their nature, have the strength and structure to break them and establish clearer and more effective ones.

Many individuals, couples and families sometimes enter into not just one but many "double-bind" contracts. "Double-bind" contracts are satisfactory to no one because the individuals who enter them feel "damned" if they try to keep them and "damned" if they do not. For example, a parent who teaches his child that he ought to come to him with his problems and then when the child comes to him with his problems feels condemned or humiliated by the parent, is in a trap or double-bind contract. The child feels guilty if he does not come or humiliated and guilty if he does come. From my experience, this is a serious mistake made not only by Christian parents but by religious leaders such as ministers, elders and Bible teachers.

A significant task of a counselor is to discover through his astute involvement with the couple or family what these contracts are. He then needs to confront these contracts. This is done primarily through the type of structure he sets up, the type of contract established and the appropriate and timely reflection (verbally and nonverbally) revealed by him in the counseling process.

Transitions Motivate Individuals to Seek Counseling

Transition (change) is a part of everyone's life. Some changes, such as aging and death are inevitable. Some changes, such as marriage, having children, moving, and changing jobs come about as a result of one's choices. While a person welcomes some changes, he also resists certain components and/or consequences of the transition. The more personal and comprehensive the change, the more likely one will resist changing. Therefore, how one views transition, as well as what he does while he is in it, largely determines whether growth occurs. Transitions vary in their impact on one intellectually, emotionally, and physically. Also, their intensity, duration, and complexity vary. Yet with all the variations, within each transition there is the opportunity for one to grow. Accompanying the potential for growth are doubt, anxiety, and a temptation for one to retreat.

Inasmuch as change is inevitable, how should one approach change? In each transition there is a time when one is lost and confused — not really knowing what to do. One of the worst things a person can do is fight being lost and confused and impulsively "do something" to avoid his frightening emotions. Once he accepts being lost and confused, faith and hope become the underlying dynamics that enables a person to work through a transition in a healthy manner.

There are changes in one's life that he alone must face and work through. This is a very critical time and it is clear that retreat is at times more inviting than continuing. It is a time when an individual must walk by faith and not by sight and a time when he does not know what the outcome will be. The more experience he has had in walking by faith, the more likely he is convinced that someway and somehow he will make it through this experience. Not only does he *expect* to make it through, but he thinks that good will result from his painful perseverance.

One of the characteristics of our society is that we are continually on the move. There are inherent problems in a mobile society. A person who is in a transient situation may discover he is also experiencing pain from other changes which are simultaneously taking place in his life. These accompanying changes may be the loss of self-esteem as a result of losing his job, the death of a loved one, reaching retirement, marital *growing pains,* separation or divorce, a loss of health (his or a family member's), the birth of a child, a child beginning school, leaving home for college, or getting married. These are just some of the many changes which may be occurring in an individual's life at the same time. Often, *when it rains, it pours!*

Individuals in today's society often find themselves to be without stable roots and close relationships. Experiencing the pain of loneliness and isolation, they tend to use considerable energy trying to avoid close ties in the church and community for fear of getting involved and then having to leave again. This approach can easily contribute to a person's being more detached from himself, family, the church, and the community. It greatly influences parents to *try* to rear children who will be able to isolate themselves from pain, intrapersonal and interpersonal involvement.

It alarms me to hear and read things from leaders in the church who are intentionally or otherwise teaching individuals to try to live without *hurting.* It is never appropriate to *inflict* pain on others. However, the inward pain inherent in living in today's society must be dealt with creatively or we in the church are going to experience more suicides, drug addicts, alcoholics and frustrated, confused and unhappy individuals.

It also disturbs me to see teachers attempting to look at the transient issue of *saying goodbye* (ending relationships and leaving surroundings which have personal meaning) often doing so in *chit-chat, chirpy* ways. I have overheard teachers, preachers, and social workers say, "Now don't cry," "Now, we're not going to talk about your leaving," "Now we aren't going to be sad today," "Today is your last day and we want it to be all smiles and no tears." I have heard these individuals choke out all feeling. In a very hollow and mechanical voice they hurriedly made a few statements about Johnny's moving or Susan's leaving as though they were pieces of machinery being shipped from one part of the country to another.

Becoming hysterical is not healthy and no one should *whine* and *wallow* in his tears, but the Bible clearly teaches when it is appropriate, a person should be sad and cry. "Jesus wept."[12] The Wise Man said, "He who sings songs to a heavy heart is like one who takes off a garment on a cold day, and like vinegar on a wound."[13] Solomon said there is "a time to weep and a time to laugh; a time to mourn, and a time to dance."[14] Paul said, "Rejoice with those who rejoice; mourn with those who mourn."[15]

Learning how to be intimate and becoming close to other significant individuals is frightening. There is also pain in a close relationship at times, especially when it ends or basic changes are made (such as moving or a child leaving home). This is due in part to so much superficial closeness in our society and the fact that individuals do not understand how to be close which involves beginning, serious modifying and ending relationships. A significant percentage of people are trying to live without relating in depth to others.

One of the fears many individuals in the church have is if an emotion is felt and acknowledged, it would automatically be expressed irresponsibly. However, if a person is truly aware of and accepts a particular emotion, he is more likely to be in control of that emotion.

Another related fear some individuals have is to be in control of oneself means feelings must be repressed or suppressed. In actuality, this causes a person to deny his feelings. Man's emotions cannot be denied successfully because they will naturally vent themselves if given enough time. If one is aware of his feelings or emotions and truly accepts them as being normal, natural, and good, he will likely be able to express them appropriately, respectfully, and responsibly. On the other hand, repressing or suppressing one's emotions is almost a guarantee they will be expressed in disrespectful and irresponsible ways. For example, anger may be turned into depression and it may be expressed through such behavior as not attending church services, pouting or physical abuse to others.

Sadness and crying may be expressed through whining, over-protection, unrealistic guilt, or becoming a hypochondriac. Affection and tenderness which cannot be expressed verbally and nonverbally may find their only outlet through sexual intercourse. A person who cannot experience good feelings of self-esteem, worth, and acceptance may become quiet and withdrawn or haughty and conceited.

Leaders need to understand the nature of relationships; how they are developed as well as how to modify or end them therapeutically. They need to take preventive and corrective measures in helping individuals understand how to grieve (say goodbye) as those who have hope as well as learn how to enter and cultivate new relationships.

It does not matter when a traumatic experience (moving, dying, etc., are traumatic experiences) occurred, it will always be present unless and until it is emotionally worked through. A person cannot work through emotional trauma without hurting. Hurting takes the form of crying, sadness, depression, fear, anxiety, doubt, questions, shame, guilt and confession. Therefore, to tell a person who had, or is having, a traumatic experience not to cry, be sad, talk about, question or be cathartic is to deny him the right to accept and deal with his problem. A person who is sad and needs to cry should never be told to cheer up, not be sad, or not cry. Notice, I did not say who is whining and feeling sorry for himself and is wanting someone to excuse and be responsible for him.

If a person is allowed to express his feelings verbally and nonverbally in a relationship of trust with an accepting, nonjudgmental person or group, he not only works through those feelings, but gets ready to become involved in other relationships. He has learned from the relationship that emotional pain is bearable, will not last forever, and really can be therapeutic. In addition, he learns valuable truths to which he can commit himself. Thus, the possibility for being a more authentic person is much greater than if he had tried to deny his feelings by not thinking about and sharing them.

A person who undergoes changes must go through certain elements of change alone. He may long for and seek out a concerned individual to be with him during the transition. The person he chooses to be with him in his struggle may be a counselor and hopefully he would discover that having someone with whom he can share his pain is both encouraging and comforting to him.

FOOTNOTES

[1]Romans 5:3-5.
[2]Hebrews 11:1.
[3]Hebrews 6:18,19.
[4]Romans 8:24,25.
[5]Proverbs 10:28.
[6]Proverbs 11:7.
[7]Proverbs 13:12.
[8]Proverbs 13:19.
[9]2 Timothy 1:7.
[10]Proverbs 27:19.
[11]Proverbs 11:22.
[12]John 11:35.
[13]Proverbs 25:20 RSV.
[14]Ecclesiastes 3:4.
[15]Romans 12:15.

Chapter 7

ENCOURAGING AND COMFORTING THE BEREAVED

How to Grieve Can Be Taught

Grieving is hard for one to do even if he knows how and is with those who understand the grief process and are willing to be with him in his grief. The sad fact is many Christians neither know how to grieve therapeutically themselves nor how to encourage and comfort the bereaved in his grief. An effective way to deal with this problem is through leaders in the church understanding that individuals can be taught how to grieve in an appropriate and adequate manner. They need to understand that the grief experience can be an ideal teaching and learning experience. Even pre-schoolers can learn how to grieve effectively.

There is a need for regular courses in grief to be taught in the Bible school. Perhaps the most effective way to teach individuals how to grieve therapeutically is by a properly trained teacher who is in the midst of a grief experience. Since there are many minor losses occurring in children's lives, there are numerous opportunities to teach children how to grieve as one having hope. Likely, greater success in teaching individuals how to grieve therapeutically lies with pre-schoolers or grade school children. This suggestion has validity because in today's society not only are individuals not taught how to grieve, but there is also a widespread denial of loss and its implications. Therefore, adults are usually too anxious to be meaningfully involved with a bereaved person as he works through his grief. Adults tend neither to mention the deceased one shortly after his death nor allow the bereaved to talk about his loved one and grieve over losing him.

Many Causes For Grief

It is probably accurate to say that in any congregation at any given time there is at least one individual in grief. Grief is the emotional experience which one has when someone or something is taken from

him. A person experiences grief when he loses a favorite toy, security blanket, pet, lim or organ; he starts to school; the school year
ends; he does or does not get promoted; he graduates; a meaningful
vacation or visit is over; a meaningful relationship changes; another
child is born into the family; a child gets married or leaves home; he
moves or retires. An individual's loss may have occurred through a
death, divorce, surgery, health, growth, retirement, fire, theft,
storm, etc. These are some of the losses an individual has and how
they occur to him. How well a person learns to grieve over his *little
losses will have a determining effect on his more significant losses.*

GRIEF IS AN OPPORTUNITY TO ENCOURAGE AND COMFORT

Christians are to encourage and comfort one another and if they
are perceptive of each other they will have many opportunities to do
so. The Hebrews writer said, "And let us consider how we may spur
one another on toward love and good deeds. Let us not give up
meeting together, as some are in the habit of doing, but let us encourage one another – and all the more as you see the Day approaching."[1] Paul said, "For you know that we dealt with each of you
as a father deals with his own children, encouraging, comforting and
urging you to live lives worthy of God, who calls you in to his
kingdom and glory."[2] He also stated, "Therefore encourage one
another and build each other up, just as in fact you are doing."[3] He
further stated, "Therefore encourage each other with these words."[4]
Paul again said, "May our Lord Jesus Christ himself and God our
father, who loved us and by his grace gave us eternal encouragement
and good hope, encourage your hearts and strengthen you in every
good deed and word."[5]

GOD MAY COMFORT THROUGH INDIVIDUALS

Often in times of grief individuals talk and pray as though God
comforts individuals in times of loss in some mysterious manner.
They seem not to be aware that the comfort which God brings individuals may be the comfort that is brought to the individual
through or by another person. Notice Paul on this point: "But God,
who comforts the downcast, comforted us by the coming of Titus,
and not only by his coming, but also by the comfort you had given
him. He told us about your affection, your deep sorrow, your ardent
concern for me, so that my joy was greater than ever."[6]

Encourage and Comfort Through Being Physically Present and Emotionally Available

When it is the helper's responsibility to reveal the heartbreaking news to another, he should do so warmly, slowly, indirectly, and kindly; giving as much time as possible for the bereaved to acknowledge his loss to himself before the helper tells him. In part, this approach is valid because it is intended to minimize the shock and aid the bereaved in experiencing his emotions about his loss. Revealing news of this nature can be damaging physically and emotionally to the bereaved.

A person will likely experience shock upon learning that he has lost a meaningful person or object. The shock or numbness an individual experiences will be in proportion to the meaning of and his dependence upon that which he has lost. His shock may last a few minutes, hours, or days. Shock is not something of which to be afraid for it is man's temporary anesthesia which God has given him to use in order to prevent his facing a grim reality all at once.

The helper should be near the bereaved at this time, but respecting his need for space – not crowding or getting in his way. The bereaved should be encouraged to share his memories about how his loss occurred, as well as permitted to be active in doing everything he can for himself.

Associated with the shocking news is denial and is seen in such expressions as, "I don't believe it," "It just couldn't have happened," "It is not so." It is appropriate at this time for the helping person to warmly and gently elicit memories which carry great emotional impact on the bereaved in order to get him in touch with his feelings. This often can be done by getting him to reminisce about the deceased. Another is through asking him to share the details about how the individual died, was killed, etc.

It is important at this point for the helper to be very sensitive about his physical presence, touch, and emotional availability. Being emotionally available means among other things, that one looks to see, listens to hear and understands in his heart the pain and struggle through which another is going. It means empathizing and being merciful and even weeping; but not losing one's objectivity. A clear example is that of Jesus as recorded in John the eleventh chapter.

The bereaved does not need to be pampered, overhugged, or clung to by the helper. Having gone through the loss of a brother, father, and mother, I am keenly aware of how valuable appropriate space, touch, and emotional availability is. On the other hand, I am aware of how uncomfortable and discouraging inappropriate touch (clinging) and individuals not being emotionally available are.

ENCOURAGEMENT AND COMFORT COMES THROUGH THE BEREAVED TALKING, FEELING AND REMEMBERING

Jesus encouraged and comforted Mary and Martha through not only being emotionally available to them, but through allowing them to express their feelings and thoughts. An individual who is experiencing grief needs to talk about his loss, as well as hear others who talk about the deceased in his presence. One of the mistakes that individuals in the church make is thinking that they are encouraging and comforting the bereaved by not mentioning the deceased or allowing the grief sufferer to talk about his loss.

When Lazarus died, "Jesus wept."[7] Paul said, "Rejoice with those who rejoice; mourn with those who mourn."[8] Solomon stated, "It is better to go to a house of mourning than to go to a house of feasting, for death is the destiny of every man; the living should take this to heart. Sorrow is better than laughter, because a sad face is good for the heart."[9]

In the early stages of grief, it is not the appropriate time to *preach* or give the bereaved too much consolation. It is usually of no value and may create problems to remind the grief sufferer to count his blessings, think how fortunate he is when compared to others and how grateful he ought to be. It is not therapeutic to try to assure the grief sufferer that "God never makes a mistake or that God does everything perfectly." It is unscriptural to tell the bereaved that he should not question God as to why his loss occurred. It is scriptural and may be appropriate to tell the grief sufferer that he can ask God any question, even "why" this has happened to him. Jesus said, "My God, my God, why have you forsaken me?"[10] If the Son of God did no sin and He asked why, then the grief sufferer can do the same. Although it is appropriate for the grief sufferer to ask why, it is not appropriate for the helper to get involved in a theological or philosophical discussion of why. This is the time for the bereaved to talk and feel − not become a student of theology or philosophy.

The real comfort the helper brings is through just letting the person talk and cry without interruption and reassuring words. The bereaved needs someone with whom he can experience his faith however strong or weak it might be. He also needs to experience the faith of the helper. He does not experience the helper's faith through detailed explanations and assurances, but through the way the helper shares his faith verbally and nonverbally. It is the way he

94

looks and listens. It is the way he warmly but deliberately talks about the deceased. It is the way he shares the pain and struggle of the grief he is experiencing, while communicating (mostly nonverbally) his courage and hope that life is still liveable. It is the way he hears and accepts the grief sufferer's doubts, guilt, questions and anxieties without being shakened and feeling the bereaved is "losing his faith." It is the naturalness with which the helper allows the bereaved to face death as a part of living. It is being the "salt of the earth"[11] and the "light of the world"[12] for another.

This is not the time for the helper to go into detail about his own grief experiences. His effectiveness will be determined largely by whether he has worked through his past grief. There is a strong temptation when another is grieving for the helper to avoid his own grief or use the bereaved to work on his past grief. Either extreme makes for "morbid grief" instead of "good grief."

The judicious use of prayer can be therapeutic at this point; however, the helper should not attempt to preach, overly assure or avoid what is really going on in his prayer. The prayer should be warm and kind, while expressing the many feelings which the bereaved is experiencing or should be experiencing at this time.

Depression and loneliness are grief reactions. The grief sufferer will likely come to feel that perhaps God is not there and does not care, others are not concerned (although they may have done numerous things), that the whole world has caved in on him, and he is isolated. He may begin to think that no one has ever grieved the way he has and is grieving. The helper may use his past depressions in a responsible way so as to give support and insight. The helping individual should talk naturally, freely, openly, and honestly about depression and loneliness. He may use a strong man like David to illustrate that others have gone through what he is going through. For example, David said,

My tears have been my food day and night, while men say to me all day long, 'Where is your God?' . . . Why are you downcast, O my soul? Why so disturbed within me? Put your hope in God, for I will yet praise him, my Savior and my God. My soul is downcast within me; therefore I will remember you from the land of the Jordan, the heights of Hermon — from Mount Mizar . . . I say to God my Rock, 'Why have you forgotten me? Why must I go about mourning, oppressed by the enemy?' My bones suffer mortal agony as my foes taunt me, saying to me all day long, 'Where is your God? Why are you downcast, O my soul? Why so disturbed within me? Put your hope in God, for I will yet praise him, my Savior and my God.[13]

Depression and loneliness are experienced after the funeral, for this is the time when everybody leaves and there is nothing to do but concentrate on grieving. There are usually physical symptoms, some of which can begin occurring before the funeral and some which are related to depression and loneliness develop after the funeral. These symptoms are: queasiness in the stomach, sharp pain in the abdomen, pounding or throbbing in the head, cottony feeling in the mouth, loss of awareness of surroundings, palpitation of the heart, sighing, feeling empty, and loss of appetite. The bereaved may even develop the physical symptoms of the deceased. It is possible for these and other physical manifestations to become more pronounced and continue for days or weeks. In fact, many people become ill because of unresolved grief.

Depression is associated with some type of loss. It may be a loss of self-esteem, employment position, a loved one, etc. Anger develops as a result of one's loss and its accompanying frustrations. Anger and frustration which are not dealt with immediately become internalized and make up a basic component of depression. As this process continues, feelings of helplessness and hopelessness emerge and the grieving person will likely begin to feel sorry for himself, want to give up and desire that others take care of him and be responsible for him. He internalizes his anger probably because he cannot keep his frustrations processed. In addition, he does not express his anger (verbally or through appropriate actions) because he is afraid, would feel guilty, embarrassed, or ashamed if he did. A person's parents, minister, or Bible school teacher may have taught him that it was wrong to get angry. Yet, he saw them when they got angry and still experiences their getting angry at times. Contradictions like these leave one confused, frustrated and may lead to apathy.

In order for a person's grieving to be therapeutic, **he must be able to express his anger** – towards himself, his loss, others and even God. Many Christians have difficulty in allowing themselves to feel their anger much less verbally express it. Therefore, this becomes a very difficult stage for them. Hostility and resentment are a part of "good grief." This is not to suggest that the helper encourage the bereaved to be hostile or resentful. One should be aware that children in particular may act out their angry feelings inappropriately instead of expressing their hostility and resentment through words. Wise indeed is the helper who through warmth, patience, and insight helps the child to accept and work through his feelings responsibly.

Anger is natural and normal. It becomes sinful when denied and irresponsibly handled. Paul said, " 'In your anger do not sin:' Do not let the sun go down while you are still angry, and do not give the devil a foothold."[14] Solomon said, " He who conceals his hatred has lying lips."[15]

If a person deals with his anger therapeutically, he must identify and specifically label it, expressing the right amount of anger responsibly and respectfully toward the appropriate person at the proper time and place. Anger is caused by unrealistic expectations of self, others and God, a feeling that one does not *fit in, belong,* or is not accepted by important others (family, peers, etc.), one's life is without purpose and meaning, a significant loss, feelings of worthlessness, love, jealousy, anxiety, frustrations, failure, permissiveness, disappointment, guilt and shame.

One of the problems a person has with his anger is whether he will express it sinfully or righteously. An individual can sin with his anger by denying he never gets angry or that he is not angry when, in fact, he is. As previously cited, Solomon said, "He who conceals his hatred has lying lips."[16] Denied anger is one underlying cause for much trouble in the home and the church. One of the tragedies in these relationships is that, most often, anger is never dealt with as anger. In attempting to deal with family or congregational discord, anger should be acknowledged as anger and dealt with as anger.

Anger is really being denied when it is given false labels as, "Well, I don't get angry, but I do feel righteous indignation at times." "A good Christian never gets angry." "I never get angry, but I sometimes get irritated." "I do not get angry with anyone at church, but I did get my feelings hurt." "I am not angry with anyone at church, but I am not coming back as long as 'so and so' is there." "I could never be angry with God."

One of the ways of helping a person to accept that being angry with God is not necessarily sinful is to use the analogy of a loving parent and child. A loving parent does not forsake or relate disrespectfully to his child when his child becomes annoyed at him. If a loving parent would not abandon or punish his child because of the child's anger, what makes one think that God, who is a loving Father, would do so? What is sinful about a person telling God that he does not like it because he has suffered a severe loss? Jesus got angry;[17] therefore, anger in and of itself is not sinful, unless Jesus sinned. An infant gets angry the first day of his life and expresses his anger, but is an infant a sinner?

Can one tell God only what he likes and that for which he is grateful? There is a marked difference between cursing God when one is angry and expressing one's true feeling of anger. It is difficult for many in the church to grasp this concept, because they may have grown up in an environment in which they saw anger expressed through curse fights, physical fights, running others down, and church splits. This difficulty may also grow out of being reared by parents who thought children were to "be seen," but "not heard," and that to question is to be disrespectful.

A child in his development naturally raises questions because that is the way God made him and it is an important way for him to learn. Why is it wrong then, for a person to respond the way God made him? Can a person ask God some questions but not others? Why? The areas in one's life in which he does not question are the areas in which he does not grow. If it is a sin to ask God "why," then Jesus sinned because He asked, "My God, my God, why have you forsaken me?"[18] Jesus quoted from David who asked:

> My God, My God, why have you forsaken me? Why are you so far from saving me, so far from the words of my groaning? Oh my God, I cry out by day, but you do not answer, by night, and am not silent.[19]

Anger really becomes dangerous when it is denied, suppressed or repressed, thus, allowing it to build up to an explosive stage. One of the sins connected with denied anger is that a person never really knows who or what makes him angry. He may not recognize that he is angry, and if he does not, he will likely charge the wrong person with the wrong thing. He usually operates in a frustrated cycle.

An individual can sin with his anger by being irresponsible with it. The question arises, "But how can one be irresponsible with his anger." By not telling another individual with whom he is angry that he is angry with him; when a person is really angry with himself, but talks and acts like he is angry only with the other individual; by "dumping" his built-up anger on another for a particular minor offense. For example: A mother has been angry about other matters all day. Her child spills his milk and mother goes into a rage over a few drops of spilled milk.

An individual is irresponsible when he expresses his anger disrespectfully. Anger, as such, and the appropriate expression of angry feelings in not disrespectful.

Anger has not been expressed disrespectfully if:

1. It has been shared without intending (consciously or unconsciously) to accuse, blame, humiliate or curse the other.

2. The individuals involved feel more self-respect and self-esteem afterwards.

3. Afterwards, a person can truthfully say that he meant what he said, as well as how expressed himself.

4. Through its expression, it leads individuals to their pain of disappointment, guilt, shame, and alienation. In addition, focusing on the pain leads them to forgiveness and reconciliation.

A person who has a hot, high or quick temper is sitting on a hot bed of anger usually will act irresponsibly or foolishly. Solomon expressed it this way.

> "A quick-tempered man does foolish things, and a crafty man is hated."[20]
>
> "A gentle answer turns away wrath, but a harsh word stirs up anger."[21]
>
> "A hot-tempered man stirs up dissension, but a patient man calms a quarrel."[22]
>
> "Do not be quickly provoked in your spirit, for anger resides in the lap of fools."[23]

An individual can sin with his anger by pouting. A pouter "swells up like a toad filled with buckshot," but his swelling is composed largely of shame and hostility which is not acknowledged openly and vented outwardly. When these feelings are turned inwardly, they produce the puffed-up effect. To camouflage his humiliation and anger, he ignores and/or withdraws from the other. He tends to be a person who whines, feels sorry for himself, thinks that others owe him something and should always agree with him. In effect, they ought to see him as a "little god."

While it is very important that individuals learn to "lead a quiet life,"[24] there is a marked difference between being quiet and pouting. A person may be appropriately quiet to relax, keep out of "another's business," to evaluate himself, the situation and what is going on, how and to what extent he wishes to be involved with another, or account for himself. However, one who is pouting does not want to account for himself, usually acts superior but feels inferior, and does not want to solve the problem but wishes to ignore it. Pouting is a forceful way of ignoring another and says that he is not worth the pouter's time and attention. The pouter sees relationships as being one way — his way. If communication is to continue, it comes through the others *bowing down* and apologizing. Sometimes a pouter may choose to start talking again if the situation changes — like people coming in, or if given enough time, his *swelling* goes down. If this happens, the pouter makes sure he begins on another subject or different *wave length,* because he definitely does not believe in giving an account as to the reason for his pouting.

Pouting is an effective way of being irresponsible with one's anger which has the makings of idolatry. If one thinks only the other should account for himself (his thoughts, words and actions) — he has already set himself up as a god.

An individual can sin with his anger by trying to force a child to *be* what he cannot. The eighteen-month or four-year-old *cannot sit still* on a church pew for an hour; yet there are leaders who encourage parents to punish their child when he is restless and cannot sit still. The punishment takes various forms:

1. Angrily *snatching* a child up by an arm and taking him out of the building for a spanking.
2. Hostilely slapping a child in the mouth or on a bare leg.
3. Putting on hard-sole shoes and then whipping the child when he moves because the shoes make noise.
4. Giving a child toys which will make noises and then spanking him because he does make noise.

All of this is done by well-meaning and sincere parents who think they are teaching their child to love God and enjoy *going to church.* Parents and other leaders need to understand that this behavior can be the beginning of a child learning that God and the *church* are rigid, cold, uncaring and cruel. Leaders need to understand that *leaving the church* can have its roots in one's infancy.

I got my share of spankings growing up and I approve of spanking a child under certain conditions. I remember being taken *out of church* for a spanking once for whistling and this was by an older brother. I also remember my mother taking quilts and blankets and spreading them out on the floor of the auditorium for the small children to quietly play and sleep on. I can still remember sitting by my mother "squirming around" because the hard pews and the long and disinteresting sermon made me uncomfortable, but she never reprimanded me. Talking and distracting others were not permissible, but quietly squirming was. I remember wondering many times during the sermon if I would ever quit squirming. I sat on an uncomfortable pew the day she was buried; I even squirmed. I see now that my mother's wisdom in this area had a profound influence on my not just being a nominal member, but committed to the Lord as I am.

An individual can sin with his anger by fussing and arguing. Anger can become a separation barrier between individuals. Unless it is clearly and specifically labeled and the focus is on the *pain* causing the separation (real or imaginary) from self and/or another, there cannot be reconciliation but further separation. Therefore, fussing and arguing can be sinful because such usually causes the separation which individuals already feel to become deeper and wider instead of their getting close together. Fussing and arguing can be a way of sinning with one's anger because it is an effective way to avoid acknowledging what one is specifically angry about, where he hurts, and what is painful. Since fussing and arguing are defenses against facing openly and honestly one's anger and its causes, it frequently generates far more anger than it releases. This buildup of anger can lead to destruction of property, physical abuse and, at times, taking another's life which, of course, are ways of sinning with one's anger.

The question naturally arises, "How can one be angry and not sin?"

1. By recognizing and accepting one's anger as anger.

2. By following the golden rule which reads, "In everything, do to others what you would have them to do to you, for this sums up the Law and the Prophets."[25] But what does it mean to follow the golden rule? I think it means that one would give serious *thought* to his anger, its causes, how, where, when and with whom he will express it, as well as be *honest* about his angry feelings and their causes and take responsibility for how he expresses them. It means responding to another out of one's anger as he would want the other person to respond to him out of his anger.

One might get angry with another person because he or she looks or talks like someone else he does not like. One might get angry at another because he or she reminds him of something in himself which he does not like. While one has the right to his angry feelings, he is being irresponsible with his anger if he simply projects his anger onto another (for whatever reason) and does not work through it.

3. By working through his angry feelings. Paul said " 'In your anger do not sin:' Do not let the sun go down while you are still angry."[26] All feelings are natural and normal and are neither moral or immoral. How one feels about, and/or where, with whom, when and how he expresses his feelings makes them moral or immoral. A person can respond to his feelings in two basic ways. He can block them out (not feel them) or he can be aware of them. My experience

has taught me that a person is more likely to sin with his feelings through blocking them out and/or accentuating one feeling to the exclusion of other feelings. Additionally, my experience has taught me that a person is more likely to sin with his feelings if he does not *think soberly* about a particular feeling and how he would feel in the light of total reality if it were expressed disrespectfully and irresponsibly. I believe a person will likely sin less and be more responsible with his feelings as he becomes aware of them, accepts them and expresses them to appropriate individuals (for example, spouse, parent) respectfully and responsibly.

The person who is depressed does not need someone to tell him to "cheer up and be thankful." In fact, such responses can make him worse, even suicidal. Solomon said, "Like one who takes away a garment on a cold day, or like vinegar poured on soda, is one who sings songs to a heavy heart."[27] The depressed individual needs someone to be with him and listen as he shares his loss and expresses his feelings of loneliness, frustration, helplessness and hopelessness. He needs someone who will be kind and firm in helping him to discover, accept and share his anger. He needs someone who will not back off or put him down as he gets in touch with his anger towards God, others and himself. Depression is indeed a dark valley through which the grief sufferer goes and often without a friend to be with him as he painfully travels through it. Pious platitudes do not help him at this time. They even can contribute to his getting stuck and remaining in this darkets of valleys.

WILL I EVER GET THROUGH?

It may take a few months, a year, two, or even longer to complete the work of bereavement. In some cases, the grief work is never completed. Therefore, the bereaved will need to talk about and cry over his loss for an extended period of time. This is much longer than society gives one to grieve. Usually an individual is given about three days to grieve and then he is expected to be about life as usual. If he does cry or show signs of sadness after this short period, individuals tend to think there is something wrong with him.

Working through one's grief is a painful struggle when accompanied by encouragement and comfort from others. Even then it is a zig-zag, up and down experience. One's grieving is never smooth and easy. Sometimes it is like taking two steps forward and then three steps backward. Eventually though, hope comes through and he can adjust and accept his irretrievable loss. Naturally one's faith is an integral component of healthy and effective grief work. Also, the helper's warmth, insight, and patience toward the bereaved will have profound influence on whether or not the grief sufferer completes his grief work.

The length of time it will take an individual to work through this grief is determined by:

1. His physical dependency on the object or person lost.

2. His emotional dependency on the object or person lost.

3. His understanding of the grief process and willingness to grieve.

4. How thoroughly and effectively he has worked through previous losses.

5. How consistently and adequately he grieves as one having hope.

6. The type and length of encouragement and comfort he receives from others.

7. The degree of anticipatory grieving he did before losing the object or person.

WRITING THIS CHAPTER HAS HELPED ME TO GRIEVE

This chapter has been a painful, but helpful one for me to write. Although I have written it while grieving, writing it has been an effective way for me to grieve. My mother died on October 26, 1980, and the same week I started lecturing on grief and writing this chapter. Since then I have given a number of lectures on grief and today, December 31, 1980, I am finishing the first draft of this chapter. Two years before, on this day, I buried my father.

I feel like I have completed my grief over the loss of a brother who was killed in an automobile accident January 15, 1965. I am just about finished with grieving over my father's death and am well into processing my grief over mother's death. The grief experience for me is one experience with which I can say with Solomon, "The end of a matter is better than its beginning, and patience is better than pride."[28]

I have resisted sharing the various degrees to which people have been helpful or have hindered my grief process. After much struggle, I share what would be considered negative responses, not to offend anyone, but hopefully to be helpful. What I share not only has come from me, but others with whom I have worked in therapy have shared the same. Individuals who have helped me the least and sometimes have hurt me through their responses have been persons who:

1. Have said they were sorry and were sympathizing with me, but their tone of voice, facial expressions, posture and gestures indicated

to me that they were just saying words; that really hurt.

2. Were afraid, at least the way they looked and acted, to say anything about my brother, father or mother to me after a few days. Of course, they did not understand what I really needed was to talk about him/her with them.

3. Were uncomfortable with my tears and did not want me to cry.

4. Looked as though they thought something was wrong with me when I cried or was sad at church weeks after the funeral.

5. Hugged too tightly or did not hug me at all.

6. Tried to comfort me through being too talkative and not just standing or sitting beside me and listening to whatever I wanted to say.

7. Tried to reassure and comfort me through quoting Scripture, telling me how fortunate I was, how grateful I ought to be or reminding me of how God takes care of his own and does not make mistakes. Sometimes this was done through prayers.

8. Warned me in a subtle way to neither question God nor let this death cause me to lose my faith.

9. Stated that I should turn to God for all my comfort, never realizing that God comforts the downcast through other Christians.

Individuals who have helped me the most were persons who neither crowded me with their words nor their touch. They seemed to listen to whatever I wanted to say and looked as though they accepted me regardless of whether I laughed or cried. These people often asked about my deceased one, and seemed to have time for me and not be in hurry when my loss was mentioned. They did not tell me to believe but listened as I shared my faith through pain, and waited for me to read the Bible largely from my memory instead of reading it to me without even asking. God has helped me through individuals and His word. I have gotten much comfort through the Scriptures but they have been passages which have emerged in me through the shock of learning that my loved one was dead, my painful loneliness, refreshing tears and loving anger. These passages were comforting because they were where I was and what I needed at that time.

Death certainly has its sting and grief is lonely, painful and time-consuming. On the other hand, it can be an ideal teaching-learning experience. Although it has been, and still is at times, very painful and difficult to keep going, I have learned some things about life, relationships and myself that I will always treasure. In one sense, I have lost in three deaths; in another sense, I think I have gained far more than I have lost.

In their deaths, I lost their physical presence, but retained their legacies; therefore, life has become richer, more meaningful and purposeful to me.

FOOTNOTES

[1]Hebrews 10:24, 25.
[2]1 Thessalonians 2:11, 12.
[3]1 Thessalonians 5:11.
[4]1 Thessalonians 4:18.
[5]2 Thessalonians 2:16, 17.
[6]2 Corinthians 7:6, 7.
[7]John 11:35.
[8]Romans 12:15.
[9]Ecclesiastes 7:2, 3.
[10]Matthew 27:46.
[11]Matthew 5:13.
[12]Matthew 5:14.
[13]Psalms 42:3, 5, 6, 9, 10, and 11.
[14]Ephesians 4:26, 27.
[15]Proverbs 10:18.
[16]Ibid.
[17]Mark 3:5.
[18]Matthew 27:46.
[19]Psalms 22:1, 2. He further asked, "Why have you rejected us forever, oh God? Why does your anger smolder against the sheep of your pasture?" (Psalms 74:1).
[20]Proverbs 14:17.
[21]Proverbs 15:1.
[22]Proverbs 15:18.
[23]Ecclesiastes 7:9.
[24]1 Thessalonians 4:11.
[25]Matthew 7:12.
[26]Ephesians 4:26.
[27]Proverbs 25:20.
[28]Ecclesiastes 7:8.

Chapter 8

COUNSELING IS A UNIQUE RELATIONSHIP

THERE IS A BIBLICAL DOCTRINE OF PSYCHOLOGY AND SOCIOLOGY

I think one of the reasons why leaders get frustrated with trying to help people solve their problems, and sometimes even give up, is because their *doctrine is too limited*. It is true that a leader should know the Biblical doctrine (or teaching) on the plan of salvation, the nature, organization and worship of the church, but it is not true that all problems with which a leader will be faced will be directly related to these areas – much less rooted in them. Some leaders seem to think that all a person, couple, or family needs to know and do is become a Christian, go to church three times a week, and refrain from such sins as lying, stealing and adultery. Thus, when a person comes to a leader with problems, he may simply tell him to do the above or something similar. It may be true that a particular person needs to obey the gospel or be more active in the church, but that may be only a part of his problem or he may have additional ones. Hence, if the other aspects of his problem or problems are not correctly identified and adequate solutions found and applied, the person will only become more confused and his problems more complicated.

I believe there is a biblical doctrine of psychology and sociology, and understanding these doctrines can significantly aid a leader in helping a person solve his problems. When I use the word *psychology* I have reference to who and what man is and *sociology* refers to one's family, community, environment, etc. If the Bible does teach a doctrine of psychology and sociology, then a leader's knowledge is not adequate if it is limited just to knowing the plan of salvation, the nature, organization, and worship of the church, etc. Unless a leader can establish from the Scripture some of the Biblical doctrines are not important, then one can assume that all Biblical doctrines are to be taken seriously because neither stands alone, but all are inter-related in God's plan for man. The Hebrews writer said:

> Therefore let us leave the elementary teachings about Christ and go on to maturity, not lay again the foundation of repentance from acts that lead to death, and of faith in God, instruction about baptisms, the laying on of hands, the resurrection of the dead, and eternal judgment. And God permitting, we will do so.[1]

THE POWER AND MEANING OF WORDS ARE ROOTED IN RELATIONSHIPS

Whatever degree of power and meaning such dynamic words as faith, hope, love, grace, mercy, justice, forgiveness, reconciliation, redemption, repentance, and confession have in a person's life they have their roots in early significant relationships. These relationships have to be recognized, accepted, understood, and dealt with if a person is going to make a significant change in his behavior and attitudes (about himself, others, and God). The more the desired change is intrapersonal and interpersonal the more these dynamics in past relationships must be dealt with in conjunction with current reality. No individual grows up without an influential environment. The more aware one is of his roots and can accept them (not deny or fight them) the more freedom he has to choose how his past will influence his present instead of control it.

TYPE OF RELATIONSHIP DETERMINES WHAT CAN BE DISCUSSED

The *type of relationship determines what can be dealt with* in the relationship as well as *to what extent*. Although many things can be suggested by the counselor, it must be understood that without the relationship those suggestions cannot be really heard by a client much less processed. Furthermore, it should be understood that both the relationship and what is dealt with are interrelated, do overlap and are important in terms of healing.

Individuals have been formed and deformed, hurt, abused and humiliated in various relationships. But, genuine Christian counseling is a unique relationship. It is a relationship of concern, openness, trust, respect, honesty, freedom, and responsibility. The training of the counselor and the contract which the two have worked out and agreed upon make such a relationship possible. Since any relationship needs proper structure, an effective counseling relationship has a structure which protects the counselor and enables the counselee to be open and honest as he shares in confidence.

FAITH, HOPE AND LOVE

Counseling is a living, sharing relationship through which corrective teaching can take place as well as further development of one's faith, hope, and love. The power and meaning (or lack of it) in these theological words are developmental and have much of their meaning in a person's early relationships. Therefore, in a client-counselor relationship that is long term, a client is enabled to have something of a corrective experience and, thus, become more nearly psychologically and theologically whole and free. If a leader does not understand this principle and function in harmony with it, he will likely discover that the more he tries to help people solve their problems the more frustrated and even exasperated he becomes.

Faith is essentially trust and commitment. It has a content and a dynamic. Its content is primarily cognitive and its dynamic is essentially developmental. Christians need a solid and adequate content and this comes by hearing and learning the word of God, but if leaders are satisfied with their followers intellectually knowing the Scripture and being able to quote numerous passages from memory, then they have not helped them to develop faith in God. "Faith without works is dead," but faith assimilated into life's experience is alive. It is not enough for Christians to quote Scripture; they must learn to live Scripture and this they do only in living relationships. This being the case, perhaps it would be wise for leaders to do less talking and more living; most followers would rather see a lesson than hear one anyway.

Hope is what anchors the client to his counselor and enables him to struggle with his counselor through various means of resistance to changing his behavior, thinking, and/or feelings. Therefore, acceptance, gradually emerging, enables him to decide more realistically whether he will adjust, modify, or eliminate a particular behavior. Acceptance also enables a person to decide if, when, and to what extent he chooses to change how he feels about himself, others, and his emotions.

Since faith is the substance of one's hope, it is essential that both the content and the dynamic be realistic and sound in order for the counselee to be able to dream, plan, and see ahead and realistically expect something constructive or healthy to come from his relationships. On the other hand, he should be able to avoid daydreaming and sheer wishful thinking, which is unrealistic.

Love is that dynamic which puts some goodness, grace, and mercy in the counselor-client relationship. I think of it as the ability to blend verbal and nonverbal communication in a harmonious manner, which is tender and warm, but firm and secure. This kind of love enables the counselor to give of himself to his client out of care and respect. Love can also allow the counselor and client to persevere responsibly in ways (verbal and nonverbal) which clearly demonstrate that the client has value and faith and hope are definite realities. To the extent a counselor works into the counseling process faith, hope, and love – and he and his client experience (intellectually and emotionally) faith, hope, and love – change is possible, whether it be behavioral and/or emotional. In addition, when these dynamics are present and experienced by each in the counseling process, they allow other components of change, such as repentance and confession, to emerge naturally.

When a counselor's motivation for counseling is characterized by faith, hope, and love and he counsels out of deep conviction, he is being an appropriate model for his client. Paul said:

> We continually remember before our God and Father your work produced by faith, your labor prompted by love, and your endurance inspired by hope in our Lord Jesus Christ. . . . You became imitators of us and of the Lord; in spite of severe suffering, you welcomed the message with the joy given by the Holy Spirit. And so you became a model to all the believers in Macedonia and Achaia.[2]

COUNSELEE DOES THE CHANGING – NOT THE COUNSELOR

An effective counselor begins where the client is (intellectually and emotionally) and allows him to change in areas wherein he wishes and at his own pace. A knowledgeable counselor knows a person cannot be helped beyond and in areas which he does not have a deep desire to change. A skilled counselor respects both his client as well as the counseling process. Realistic growth is *up and down, zig-zag, back and forth,* but on a graph one can see that overall there is progress, or movement, forward.

A counselor may pressure his client to grow faster than he is growing; but if he does, he will likely frustrate both his client and the growth process. Some reasons why a counselor may pressure his client and the growth process are:

1. He may neither understand nor respect the process. It takes time for certain dynamics to become operative and, once functioning, it takes time for pain to get worked through and healing to take place.

2. He may feel that he must not only tell, but demand his client to change what he wants him to and at the counselor's pace.

3. The client may be in an area in which the counselor has not worked before and may be creating more anxiety, guilt, or shame in the counselor than he wishes to feel.

4. The counselor may be *in over his head* and does not know what to do. He may even fight with or blame his client and/or focus on justifying himself and what he is doing or has done.

UNDERSTANDING THE NATURE OF CHANGE

In counseling, change is an ongoing process in which a client is actively and/or passively involved (sometimes more one way than the other). Therefore, the counselee is not static and stale. In the change process the client moves forward by questioning, testing (the structure and the counselor), and criticizing. He continues the process by regressing (through memory and emotion into past experiences), interpreting, struggling, giving up and letting go as his vision of change becomes clearer and more definitely focused, he ceases fighting against his emotions, self, and conditions and reflectively acts upon his interpretations. This being true, a client seldom experiences a *major change;* however, when change does occur, it usually is *minor.* Viewed from this perspective, conversion is not a one-time experience, which is static and stale, but is an ongoing process which at times is (what might be called) more secular than religious and vice versa and personal rather than interpersonal (for example: marital, family).

If conversion means change, if growth necessitates change, and if Christians are exhorted to grow (change), then obviously there is more than one type of conversion discussed in the New Testament. Naturally, a person is *born again* only once, but there are many conversions (changes) which a growing Christian will experience in his maturation process. The New Testament clearly teaches faith, repentance, and confession are essential components in any change which the Christian experiences in his growth process with baptism being a component of change only in the new birth.

An analogy of the new birth is sometimes illustrated as steps into a building (hear, believe, repent, confess, and be baptized) and has value in the teaching-learning process. It can be misleading if a person perceives these dynamics (with the exception of baptism) as being practiced only by the alien sinner and then only once. In reality, the Christian becomes more Christlike as he walks by faith, and the frequency of his repenting and confessing (to himself, God, and/or others) is determined by such factors as:

111

1. Frequency of his mistakes or sins.
2. Redirecting his life after his sins.
3. Clearer focusing on his problem areas and growth potential.
4. Deeper and more commitment to the Lord.

According to what some individuals have shared with me, whether intentional or otherwise, the impression has been left with some Christians that since they have heard, repented, confessed and been baptized, there is little, if anything, left for them to do except to go to church three times a week and not do such things as lie, steal, murder, commit adultery, etc. Some Christians tend to feel their focus in private conversations, sermons, and Bible classes, should be primarily, if not altogether, focused on the lost. The lost definitely need to be converted; but individuals with similar attitudes as described above seem not to be aware or understand that the components hear, believe, repent, and confess are inherent dynamics not only in becoming a Christian, but also in daily living as one.

Experience – An Effective Teacher?

Counseling helps a person to make sense out of and learn from his experiences. One common problem which many people have, both in and out of the church, is trying to make sense out of their lives, marriages, families, vocations, experiences, and find meaning and purpose in them. It is not enough for a leader to tell a person in such a search what or how to do – if they have grown up in the church they have probably heard the *what* and *how* (though probably vague and overly simplistic) many times before coming for counseling. If such has not worked heretofore, it is likely not going to help now, but will probably frustrate the individual even more and leave him with an even greater sense of a lack of understanding of himself and his situation, meaning, and purpose in his life. The only effective way that I know to help an individual in this condition is by helping him to discover and make sense out of his own experiences and from such find meaning and purpose for his life.

Some individuals accept the inaccurate view that experience is not only a good teacher, it is one's best teacher. Experience *per se* is not a guarantee that a person is learning anything of a constructive nature. To illustrate, an alcoholic has probably drunk for years and repeated the process of buying a fifth, getting drunk, and sobering up many times. He may have had years of experience in this practice; but who would say that he learned anything constructive through his daily or weekly drinking? It would perhaps be accurate to say that he learned little, if anything, constructive from his drinking. It seems to me that experience was not necessarily a good teacher for him, and certainly not his best teacher.

Experience, then, is not always a *good* teacher, much less one's *best* teacher. A person may not learn anything constructive or helpful from his experiences. An individual may experience the same thing for ten years or he may have ten years of experience. It can be said with certainty that experience does make a permanent impression — whether constructive or destructive.

I am convinced that experience is an effective teacher to the degree that:

1. One is open to it.
2. Correctly understands it.
3. Properly interprets it in relation to the various aspects of reality in the context in which it occurs.
4. Constructively learns from it.

Counseling is a relationship in which a client can be helped in analyzing and interpreting his experiences and potentially counseling can be an effective teaching method. Therefore counseling is a relationship in which a client can learn to interpret his experiences more accurately.

A client's past experiences are important and he needs to make sense out of them, but he is also having significant experiences daily. An effective counselor focuses on both the past as well as one's current experiences. Rather than ignore these experiences or superficially respond with a quick reference to such passages as Romans 8:28, a wise counselor seeks to help his client learn how to focus on them. This can be done through such questions as "What does this mean to you?", "What are you learning from this?", "How can this experience be used to help you live a more effective and meaningful life?" There are times when a counselor can most effectively teach by focusing respectfully and appropriately on current experiences of his client. To illustrate, when a counselee is laughing, a counselor might focus in a gentle, kind, open, and sincere manner on laughter. The same would apply to boredom, anger, tears, or whatever his counselee is experiencing.

Nine valuable reasons for correctly understanding and properly interpreting experiences, verbal and nonverbal, which are taking place in clients, are:

113

1. Many people never learn to analyze, evaluate, and make sense out of what is happening in their lives. This leads to frustration, boredom, and meaninglessness. A skilled counselor is able to help the individual recognize, understand, and assimilate the psychological, sociological, and theological issues which are emerging within a person and/or the group on a verbal and nonverbal level. By so doing, a counselee gradually begins to learn how to analyze and make sense out of his experiences and correctly interpret them for himself.

2. When current experiences are interpreted, it forces a counselee to deal with what is happening *here* and *now;* this makes the data current and alive and easier for him to understand.

3. When current experiences are being correctly interpreted, it forces a client to deal with himself and what is going on in the room instead of getting focused on issues and individuals outside the counseling setting.

4. This method of teaching forces a client to talk about theology, psychology, sociology, etc, in terms of himself and what is happening to him.

5. Focusing on one's current experiences enable him to see the Bible and God are relevant to his life in the present tense. So many people spend their time talking about the past, other people, or the future without knowing how to relate directly to the present and themselves. After a person has operated this way for years, it is no wonder he has serious difficulty learning how to live authentically in the present. This method of teaching is a way of realistically assisting an individual in truly learning how to live each day of his life a day at a time.

6. Focusing on one's experiences helps a counselee recognize, understand, and learn how to deal with issues as they are developing. There is not a long period of time between the time he says or does something and the time in which he is made aware of it. He learns how to live a less frustrating and more rewarding life.

7. It can be a practical way of helping a person learn how to be angry and not sin, but at the same time get rid of his anger before the sun goes down. Paul said, "In your anger do not sin: do not let the sun go down while you are still angry, and do not give the devil a foothold."[3] Solomon said, "He who conceals his hatred has lying lips, and whoever spreads slander is a fool."[4]

8. Focusing on one's experiences forces a person not only to deal with verbalization, but to get down into the heart of the issues and

focus on them. Thus, an individual begins to learn how to grow as a person; and this current growing, which is experienced by him, is motivation for him to continue to grow. One of the reasons why it is so difficult to keep people motivated is that they do not experience in personal, meaningful, specific ways how what they are saying, doing, or being is of value to them in terms of meeting their needs and interests.

9. Helping a counselee make sense out of and learn from his experiences has the potential of continually encouraging and motivating him to grow further because he is essentially always experiencing reality in the present. He learns something of what he is saying, doing, or being is valuable, meaningful, and worthwhile to him.

Individuals are formed and deformed in relationships over a long period of time, and it is in relationships where persons *unlearn* ineffective patterns of relating and incorrect personal concepts as well as relearn inherent components of their personalities and effective ways of relating interpersonally. Counseling is both a relationship and teaching method in furthering a person's appropriate self-worth and realistic growth.

A STRUGGLE FOR MEANING AND PURPOSE

Counseling is a relationship in which a person can struggle for meaning and purpose in his life. One reason why a person may come for counseling is because his life has lost its meaning and purpose. Meaning and purpose are two concerns which emerge early in a person's life. Although a person may not be aware of it and cannot articulate it, he is in search of meaning and purpose throughout his life. Naturally, the degree, depth, and clarity will vary considerably with individuals as well as with the same individual at different times in his life.

The word for meaningless occurs 79 times in the Old Testament, 40 of which occur in Ecclesiastes. It means no profit, advantage or gain; that which does not count or matter; it yields no profitable results. It is aimless, fruitless, emptiness, transitory; having no real substance. A word which summarizes the above and fits with the context of how meaningless is used in Ecclesiastes is coherence.

Solomon acknowledges in Ecclesiastes that everything is meaningless. Wisdom, pleasures, folly, toil, oppression, friendlessness, advancement and riches are meaningless in and of themselves. They make sense and become truly profitable for a person as he can blend them into his lifestyle. In coherence there is a blending together so that they function harmoniously. Lasting coherence grows out of being centered in God *who is reality.*

Although meaning and purpose (goal, aim) are not the same, they are interrelated. An individual may have a purpose without being coherent, but he cannot be coherent without a purpose. A person needs purpose in his life to find meaning or become coherent and maintain it. An individual needs purposes which are based on reality as well as being realistically achievable.

While a person needs to be coherent and purposeful, growth requires an individual to become incoherent (lost) at times. However, through purpose he again becomes coherent. Incoherence or loss of meaning can also come as a result of change over which one has no control. Futhermore, secondary incoherences are neither as threatening nor require as much knowledge, time and effort to work through and become coherent again as primary ones.

To have a deep and abiding sense of meaning, one must have an adequate set of primary and secondary purposes which are not conflictual, but are complimentary. They must be based on reality and attainable, although it may take considerable struggle and time to accomplish them. A person must have the ability and commitment to set a goal. Once this is done, he should focus on the process and not the goal. Occasional reflection on one's goal(s) is helpful, but to think and talk of it often is to avoid the process which is absolutely necessary to achieving one's goal(s).

One of the goals or purposes for therapy is that of helping a person make sense out of his nonsense. It is helping an individual *get things together* in order to become coherent.

WORK OUT YOUR SALVATION WITH FEAR AND TREMBLING

Counseling is a relationship in which a person can continue to work out his salvation with fear and trembling. Paul said, "Therefore, my dear friends, as you have always obeyed—not only in my presence, but now much more in my absence—continue to work out your salvation with fear and trembling."[5] There are issues, questions, and problems in terms of one's salvation relating to himself, his marriage, family, vocation, church, God, which are so complex and frightening that he may very well need a concerned and informed counselor to help him in not only recognizing, but dealing with such matters appropriately and adequately. As Paul exhorted and encouraged the Philippians, leaders today need to take him seriously and follow his example. I am convinced that a number of individuals who have given up on working out their salvation would still be continuing if their leaders had encouraged them soon enough to seek professional help in working out their salvation with fear and trembling.

LEARNING TO ACCEPT AND BE ONESELF

Counseling is a relationship in which a person can discover, accept and be himself if he chooses. Some individuals suffer unduly because they are trying to be someone they are not!

One problem an individual may have is a fear of discovering himself. This fear is rooted in his believing that self is basically corrupt and/or unlovable. This person may have spent and does spend much time and energy, likely everyday, trying to avoid knowing certain parts of himself. He lives with haunting anxiety that should he ever really discover himself he would be so overwhelmed that he would actually be devoured.

Becoming oneself does not mean blaming others for ones mistakes, but it does mean accepting and being responsible for oneself. A client frequently wants the counselor to take responsibility for him. This is seen in such expressions as: "Tell me what to do", "What would you do?", "I do not know how to get my children to behave—you tell me—you are the expert", "Coming to you is not helping because you never tell me what to do", "At least you could tell me what is wrong with me", "I don't know what I am feeling—you tell me."

A real temptation for some unskilled and haughty counselors is thinking that they can be responsible *for* clients. A wise and skilled counselor knows that he cannot be responsible for his client but he will commit himself to being responsible *to* and *with* his client. Often a counselor who tries to be responsible for his counselee will end up not being responsible *for* himself and irresponsible *with* his counselee. Sometimes his irresponsiblity is very serious.

DIFFERENTIATING FAILURE AND MISTAKE

Individuals who come for counseling usually do not come because they feel successful. They are more likely to come out of feeling some sense of failure.

Often a sense of failure which motivates people to seek counseling in part grows out of their loss of balance or correct perspective of themselves and life. They may have focused on their thoughts to the exclusion of their feelings or their feelings to the exclusion of their thoughts. They may have confused their fantasies with reality. They may have a history of acting impulsively rather than intentionally. They may have lost the ability to laugh at themselves, as well as share their sadness. They may have pretended with each other instead of being honest with one another. They may have thought by forgetting and not remembering their discord that they would eventually live in harmony with each other. They may have thought that running from their problems was solving them. They may have pretended if they would not talk about their pain it would go away. They may have thought focusing on ideals, shoulds, and should nots would somehow deal with what is or reality. They may have thought that if they would never say anything upsetting to one another neither would have a reason to be upset and would, therefore, never get upset.

These and similar imbalances or incorrect perspectives of individuals and their relationships motivates some to seek help and others to seek a way out through giving up. Giving up may take the form of passivity, lukewarmness, drugs, divorce, or even suicide. When leaders look at this reality clearly and seriously, surely they must ask what contribution, if any, they have made. Perhaps they should consider that rigid, overly simplistic and idealistic rules contribute to an imbalance in individuals and their relationships.

A counselor and/or his client can confuse failure and mistake also. Success and failure are two very powerful words in American culture. Often they are defined in narrow and materialistic terms. This type of approach may neither deal thoroughly with the areas covered nor include vital ones. This being the case, a person can easily have an erroneous concept of success or failure. This simplistic approach contributes to individuals thinking that monetary success assures personal, marital, family and spiritual success.

It is important for both a counselor and his client to make a clear distinction between a mistake and failure. Dynamically speaking, failure implies finality and totality. Therefore, forgiveness, correction, reconciliation, and hope are not possible. Mistake carries with it the idea of stumbling, neglecting or not measuring up. It implies that an error in judgment was made in relation to a specific decision, problem, or situation. Therefore, adjustment, modification, correction, forgiveness, reconciliation, improvement, and hope are definite realities. If a counselor or client chooses to, he can look at his mistake analytically, deal with it responsibly and at the same

118

time, accept the consequences of it without blaming others or excusing himself. Obviously, both counselor and counselee may need some help in dealing appropriately and adequately with a mistake.

One of the most serious mistakes which a counselor or counselee may make is that of being *unaware or ignorant of his mistakes.* A mistake is most likely not a failure, but a succession of mistakes can add up to be failure.

The more a counselor learns through understanding why, when, where, and what caused him to make a mistake with a client the more successful he will be in working with individuals. As a counselor, he does not deal with what *should be* but with *what is.* Some leaders avoid the *what is* and focus on the *what should have been* or *should be* which is of no real value to the client who is currently needing help with *what is.* This approach usually leads a client in getting further and further away from health and wholeness.

Another costly mistake a counselor can make is that of being arrogant. He may not know what he is doing while pretending with his client that he does. It would be so much better if he could just acknowledge to himself and his client that he does not know what he is doing in a given area. A counselor needs to be as honest with himself and his client as Paul was with the Romans. He said, "I do not understand what I do. For what I want to do I do not do, but what I hate I do."[6] One perhaps unconscious failure a leader can make is that of continuing to do what he hates doing without being honest with himself and his clients. To illustrate, how many times has a leader met with someone or *had the phone to his ear* while just being irritated with what he was doing? How much better it would be for him in a loving, honest, non-attacking manner saying something like, "I just have gotten myself in a trap and I do not like what I am doing", or "You caught me at a time when I am busy. I can only give you two minutes but I will be glad to give you those."

Success in helping people is like putting a large puzzle together when all the pieces have been scrambled and the picture on the front of the box has faded and pieces of it torn away. Some of the pieces the client must put together himself; others, the counselor will help him find where they go. But they seldom work in one place for long at a time. Counseling is like looking at pieces over and over, finding one piece here and there that will fit; reflecting, rethinking, and looking again until finally the *puzzle* has been put together.

The most successful a counselor may be with a given case is knowing he did not hurt his client. It becomes very important for a

119

person to know and accept his limitations and make appropriate referrals. If leaders knew and accepted their limitations and made appropriate referrals many Christians would be spared much misery and perhaps sometimes loss of physical and spiritual health. Success in helping a client deal with his mistakes begins and continues with a counselor recognizing, accepting, and responsibly dealing with his own mistakes.

FOOTNOTES

[1]Hebrews 6:1-3.
[2]Thessalonians 1:3, 1:6, 7.
[3]Ephesians 4:26, 4:27.
[4]Proverbs 10:18.
[5]Philippians 2:12.
[6]Romans 7:15.

Chapter 9

COMMUNICATION – A MEANS OF GROWING SPIRITUALLY

WHAT DOES BEING SPIRITUAL MEAN?

Being spiritual means different things to different individuals. To some it is a ritual – the performance of which is more out of custom than a sincere expression of what is in one's heart. To others it is a meaningless ritual coupled with refraining from certain worldly pleasures. Some seem to think spirituality is being nice and polite regardless of how they feel and what they think. While there are certain acts to be performed, the performance as such is not spirituality.

Spiritual is related to the word *spirit* and spirit means wind or breath. There are a number of passages which clearly teach that one's spirituality springs from breathing out or sharing the *truth* which is within his heart. "And the Lord God formed man from the dust of the ground and breathed into his nostrils the breath of life, and man became a living being."[1] In this passage, breath is synonymous with spiritual. Jesus said to the Samaritan woman, "Yet a time is coming and has now come when the true worshipers will worship the Father in spirit and truth, for they are the kind of worshipers the Father seeks. God is spirit, and his worshipers must worship in spirit and truth."[2] Paul said, "Therefore, I urge you, brothers, in view of God's mercy, to offer yourselves as living sacrifices, holy and pleasing to God – which is your reasonable worship."[3]

A Christian needs to be careful lest he become like the people in both Isaiah's and Christ's day when they said, "These people honor me with their lips, but their hearts are far from me."[4] Paul admonished, "Whatever you do, work at it with all your heart, as working for the Lord, not for men."[5]

Christ is truth personified and the Bible is truth revealed. He said, "I am the way and the truth and the life."[6] To the Jews who had believed him, Jesus said, "If you hold to my teaching, you are really my disciples. Then you will know the truth, and the truth will set you free . . . so if the Son sets you free, you will be free indeed."[7]

THE BIBLE IS A SPIRITUAL BOOK

If the Scriptures are spiritual writings and if one's spirituality is based on the degree that he practices, assimilates or lives by the Scriptures, then one is being spiritual to the degree that he applies (digests) the Scriptures to himself, his situations, problems, questions, and intrapersonal and interpersonal relationships.

A variety of ways of being spiritual is dealt with in the Scriptures and there are a variety of ways a person can be spiritual in applying Scripture. This being the case, it is possible for a person to be spiritually strong in certain areas of his person and relationships and be sinful, weakly, and sickly in others.

Since the Bible is a spiritual book, any communication in it regarding the human condition or relationships is spiritual. Therefore, when an individual is communicating (as will be discussed) with himself, God or others, he is being spiritual.

Just because one can potentially sin through eating the Lord's Supper does not mean that he should not participate. One can sin sexually, with his anger or with his sadness. Nevertheless, he should still communicate with himself, God and others regarding these emotions. In fact, failure to communicate verbally and nonverbally one's sexual feelings, anger or sadness can be a way of moving a person to sin with these emotions through inappropriate behavior. Not only is appropriate communication of one's feelings spiritual, it is an effective way of helping an individual to keep from sinning with his feelings through improper behavior and attitudes. Inappropriate attitudes are the feeling patterns that individuals have learned about themselves and their emotions which are neither scriptural nor realistic. Individual Christians sometimes develop attitudes which impede their spiritual growth and contribute to their spiritual death.

WHAT ONE FEELS ABOUT HIS EMOTIONS MAY CAUSE HIM MORE DIFFICULTY THAN HIS EMOTIONS DO

If one accepts the Bible as revealed truth, then he must accept that God made man with emotions. In his developmental process a person may have learned:

1. To be ashamed of his emotions, especially his need to give and receive affection genuinely both verbally and nonverbally.

2. To be afraid of his emotions. He fears his own anger, affectionate and sexual feelings. He may be afraid because in the past he expressed them disrespectfully and irresponsibly. He may be afraid because he thinks if he allows himself to feel them, he would be overwhelmed and would act inappropriately and irresponsibly.

3. To feel guilty when his emotions emerge. His guilt may come from believing that to feel or think something is as bad as doing it. It may come from believing *he should not* have certain feelings; therefore, if he does he is sinning. His guilt may come from *acting out* in the past and he does not want to deal with those painful feelings. It may come from believing that to *talk out* a feeling is the same as *acting it out*. In the past a person may have *talked about* a feeling and then *acted it out* and because of the experience confused the two.

TALKING OUT FEELINGS CAN LEAD TO ACTING OUT FEELINGS INAPPROPRIATELY

One of the concerns which leaders have, and rightly so, is whether or not counseling is spiritual. I am convinced that genuine Christian counseling not only is spiritual, but it can teach a person how to deepen his spirituality as well as how to share it more effectively. This is said with the understanding that *sharing one's thoughts and feelings has its dangers*. Leaders need to clearly perceive and teach their followers that:

1. There are different levels of interpersonal communications.

2. Sharing which is welcomed and accepted on one level may be unwanted and would be rejected by the same person on another level.

3. Intellectual sharing of ideas and abstract concepts is different from sharing personal thoughts and feelings about oneself.

4. Sharing one's thoughts and feelings about another person is not the same as sharing thoughts and feelings about oneself.

Sharing without awareness of these factors and/or out of confusion about them has caused many individuals to suffer severe pain (embarrassment, guilt, rejection, disappointment, anxiety, etc.). As a result they have concluded that sharing is of no value and should be avoided. Much of what goes on in some congregations, marriages and families is the talking about intellectual and abstract concepts, as well as speaking in the second and third persons. While at the same time intrapersonal and interpersonal loneliness, alienation and isolation gradually but consistently and painfully increases.

124

The *nature* and *strength* of a relationship are two key factors which help determine *what* is shared, as well as *to what extent* and *when* it is shared. It is unwise to share everything with a spouse in just any manner, under any circumstances, and at any time. Sharing, even in marriage, should be on the basis of trust, respect, openness, honesty, concern, responsibility and filled with *grace* and *salt*. There should be solid reasons for sharing in any relationship. The sharer who truly benefits himself through his communications shares out of choice and intentionally. A person who *talks* impulsively rarely experiences intimacy and then only briefly. Each need has different levels. Intimacy which results from meeting a need on a given level neither insures other needs being met satisfactorily nor that the same need would automatically be met on a deeper level.

1. **Talking out feelings may lead to acting out feelings inappropriately if one does not trust himself and the person with whom he is talking.** Trust grows out of working through one's doubts and questions. Solomon said, "I applied my heart to what I observed and learned a lesson from what I saw."[8] A person who thinks that he truly trusts himself and the individual with whom he is talking without good reasons is really *blind* and is likely acting impulsively or talking obsessively and compulsively. Solomon said, "A simple man believes anything, but a prudent man gives thought to his steps."[9]

Doubts and *questions* are inherent in one's learning to *trust* himself, others and his environment. When a child's environment is essentially safe and dependable, he is naturally inquisitive. He is going to explore his environment to see what is in it and how it works.

Much of what parents may do in the name of discipline during the early years destroys the child's desire to know, question, test and discover. When a child is sufficiently *punished* (through constant harsh nos, slaps on hands and spankings) long enough, he loses much of his desire to question and discover. Being less interested in learning for himself, he may conform to parental and societal pressures (often called wishes). Strangely enough, he is often rewarded for not asking questions and testing his limits. He may often hear, "my Johnny is the best child, when I ask him to do something he never asks why." "Susan has always been so good . . . she does exactly what I say, never giving me a minute's trouble." "It did not take but a few spankings before I could leave Bill in the kitchen, living room or anywhere and he would not touch a thing."

There are various reasons why parents do not want their child to question them and explore their environment. Such may be tiring, frustrating, aggravating, embarrassing and guilt producing for the parents. They may see questions and the desire to learn as being essentially *bad* — meaning, their child is being *deliberately destructive* and will grow up to be irresponsible as well as irreligious. Parents may not make the distinction between a child *tearing up something* or asking questions because he *wants to know* and *defying* them. They many not understand that a child who loses (through punishment) his desire to explore and discover and his interest in his environment may not be interested in learning about God and life later.

There are parents and religious leaders who want children to learn so long as the children are willing to listen and agree with them. They do permit children to ask a few questions provided they:

a. Ask them *when* the adults want them to.

b. Make the adults *look good* (boost their egos) to themselves and others. Adults likely never tire of children complimenting them. They do seem to easily tire of complimenting their children, especially for *wanting to know.*

c. Are simple and the adults already know the answers and will not have to think or struggle.

Adults and religious leaders may not like for children to ask them questions if:

a. They think the children are disagreeing with them. A person may disagree with another for a number of reasons without being disrespectful. He may:

(1.) Not understand what the other means by what he says.

(2.) Not agree because he does not understand how such would satisfactorily meet a particular need of his at a specific level.

(3.) Be bored and wants to break his boredom.

(4.) Want to argue as a means of getting out his hostility and/or feel important.

b. They ask them something they do not know. Some adults pretend to children they know everything.

c. Their questions reveal they are doubting God and/or some value they have been taught. In one's growth process it is natural to doubt and question God and certain values at times. *Blindly* following is not the way to develop trust. A skilled counselor helps provide the relationship, appropriate questions and patience wherein a client can answer *his* questions and *work through his doubts.*

2. **Talking out feelings may lead to acting out feelings inappropriately if one is ashamed, afraid and/or feels guilty when talking about them.** This is more likely to happen if a person has considerable buildup of *shame,* fear, guilt and/or anger due to:

a. His low self-esteem or low self-worth.

b. An unrealistic, contradictory, inadequate and vaguely defined value system.

c. Not getting his various needs met on different levels in an adequate and consistent manner.

d. Having never learned to share his feelings discreetly.

e. Thinking that behavior regarding one need will automatically meet another need. For example, a person may need affection and to be esteemed. He may think illicit sexual intercourse will meet this need for affection and self-worth.

3. **Talking out feelings may lead to acting out feelings inappropriately if one is experiencing intrapersonal and interpersonal alienation, isolation and loneliness.** This probability is in proportion to:

a. The degree to which the various aspects of one's self are integrated.

b. The frequency a person experiences genuine intrapersonal and interpersonal relating which meets his needs satisfactorily.

c. The intensity which an individual is hungering and thirsting for a need to be met.

4. **Talking out feelings may lead to acting out feelings inappropriately if shared with an inappropriate person, place and time.** It would likely be unwise for a teenager who is aroused sexually and is also lonely and experiencing low self-esteem to discuss his sexual feelings with this girlfriend/boyfriend when they are in a place where they easily could and would have ample time to engage in sexual contact. It would be wise for him to discuss them with his parents, minister or counselor at a later time. When one is experiencing anger towards another just before public worship begins, it is probably neither the time nor place to share his angry feelings.

5. **Talking out feelings may lead to acting out feelings inappropriately if:**

a. **talking about them is just for the purpose of arousal;** this has validity whether the feeling is sexual, anger, fear, jealousy, etc;

127

b. **one has mixed motives;** he is saying one thing but his real purpose is different from what he is saying;

c. **he is talking about one feeling to the exclusion of other feelings.**

There are two ways of approaching feelings which can be dangerous:

(1.) Blocking them out through suppression and repression which lead to their *buildup*. Feelings can build to a point where they control a person instead of him controlling his feelings. When one is not aware of his feelings, they tend to come out in disguised ways which he neither understands nor can control.

(2.) Allowing one feeling to be aroused to the point that he is not aware and in control of his other feelings. When this happens a person also tends to be unaware of what he would feel later if he acted out this particular feeling while excluding the others. A person in this condition usually acts more impulsively than intentionally. He acts and then feels regretful instead of thinking before he acts. The clearer one's understanding of his emotions and the more appropriately he expresses them, the less *sinner* he is and the more *saint* he becomes.

ONE NEEDS TO BE WHOLE

Genuine growth of the whole person requires one to face and come to grips with reality or truth. An individual cannot face and deal with every aspect of reality at one time. Growing in a given area necessitates accepting and dealing with the reality in that area. One way to avoid reality is to focus on *should* or *should nots* instead of *what is*. Another way is thinking that a person is like a blank sheet of paper. Each day he starts over and his past has no influence on his present. Therefore, one should not think about, much less consider, his past.

Emotions are a part of reality and the absence of feeling is numbness. Paul affirmed that one's conscience can be seared.[10] As a person grows (becomes less seared) intrapersonally in the area of pain, he will to a greater depth genuinely experience his joy. If a person cannot feel his sorrow, he cannot feel his joy in depth. If an individual cannot feel the pain of childbearing or being married, he cannot deeply feel the joys which come from these relationships. A lack of feeling leads to phoniness and deception of self and others.

To sear one's heart from pain is to sear it from joy also. Solomon said there is "a time to weep and a time to laugh"[11] but the sad reality is that some individuals can neither weep nor laugh.

Most Christians I see have more of a problem with what they feel about their God-given emotions than the emotions themselves. A Christian who thinks that he should never be anxious is likely going to have a much greater problem with anxiety, which is natural and normal under certain conditions. An individual who thinks he should never have any sexual thoughts or feelings may end up with guilt, compulsive masturbation, promiscuity, frigidity and impotence. A Christian who never experiences his sadness in its season may end up having much more of a problem with depression, self-pity, and hopeless feelings than he would have thought possible if he could have only experienced his sadness in its season. An individual who is ashamed to acknowledge and share his pain or hurt will likely end up feeling bitter, resentful, sarcastic and arrogant.

SPIRITUALITY IS MORE THAN PERFORMING CERTAIN ACTS

Since religious leaders have long emphasized spirituality as performing certain acts, some Christians have concluded that one can be spiritual only when he is engaging in those acts in a certain ritualistic place and pattern. It is relatively easy for Christians to become like the Samaritans; Jesus said about them, "You Samaritans worship what you do not know."[12] Just being traditional is a way of guaranteeing one's spiritual death.

A much deeper understanding and dynamic growth in the five avenues of worship (teaching, singing, giving, communion, and praying) are seriously needed. Comparatively speaking, one reason is that the church has hardly begun to realize, much less maximize, depths and heights into which Christians could grow through these avenues. The avenues are sound; the problem is a lack of awareness and depth of insight accompanied with getting bogged down in traditions, which themselves restrict and limit one's spiritual growth.

I am moving away from tradition when I say that sound Christian counseling is an effective method in teaching a person something of what being spiritual means, as well as how to share his spirituality. If what the inspired writers wrote was spiritual, then a Christian is being spiritual to the degree that he assimilates, or applies, Scripture to himself and his relationships. *I believe the core of one's spirituality lies in the type and degree of his communication with himself, with God and others.* This is a simple, but very profound and complex statement. Simply stated, *spiritual communication is sharing the truth which is in one's heart and receiving the truth which another shares from his heart.* It is relatively easy to misunderstand what both God and one's fellowman are sharing. Therefore, one reads and rereads Scripture to be sure he understands what God is saying to him. In effective interpersonal communication one considers carefully *what* he hears and *how* he hears it. Appropriate feedback is given to determine whether the individuals attempting to communicate are on the same level as well as being precisely understood.

NINE COMPONENTS OF AN EFFECTIVE SPIRITUAL
COMMUNICATION

Although the following points are related and do overlap, the quality of spirituality in a given intrapersonal or interpersonal communication is affected by the degree to which each of these components is present in a specific communication. A person can be spiritual to a degree and in certain areas without listening to and having fellowship with other individuals. However, his spiritual maturing is based on sharing truth with God and others, as well as being creatively involved in listening to and jointly participating with God and other individuals. Effective spiritual communication consists of at least nine interrelated components.

1. *"Speaking the truth in love."*[13] It is possible for a person to be "always learning, but never able to acknowledge the truth."[14] Many individuals have a problem with speaking the truth. They seem to prefer being closed and deceptive rather than open and truthful. Often the truth is not shared until it is shared in a blaming, condemning manner; then, truth has been mixed with contaminants and ceases to be unadulterated truth. Many individuals are given to hearsay and assumption. This confirms Solomon's statement, "Gold there is, and rubies in abundance, but lips that speak knowledge are a rare jewel."[15] Nevertheless, individuals need to take seriously that God desires truth in the inner parts. Notice! "Surely you desire truth in the inner parts; you teach me wisdom in the inmost place."[16]

To be spiritual one must speak the truth, but it must be spoken in love. If that is the case, it will be spoken with sincerity, patience and kindness.[17] Solomon said, "A man's wisdom gives him patience; it is to his glory to overlook an offense."[18] He also said, "Through patience a ruler can be persuaded, and a gentle tongue can break a bone."[19] It should be clearly understood when the truth is spoken in love, it frees an individual. Therefore, speaking the truth in love is a way of being spiritual.

2. *Sharing truth sincerely.* Digested truth makes for sincerity or congruence. Peter said: "Now that you have purified yourselves by obeying the truth so that you have sincere love for your brothers, love one another deeply, from the heart. For you have been born again, not of perishable seed, but of imperishable, through the living and enduring word of God."[20]

3. *Sharing truth specifically.* One of the reasons why individuals are no more spiritual than they are in their marriages, families, and congregations is they tend to speak in vague, ambiguous, and general terms. They talk around the truth rather than share it directly, clearly and specifically. Individuals can tire themselves through speaking without ever sharing themselves. Jesus was able to be specific in His responses to others. In responding to the Samaritan woman's interest in the Messiah, Jesus said, "I who speak to you am he."[21] In responding to the question of the expert in the law regarding what he must do to inherit eternal life, " 'What is written in the law?' he (Jesus) replied. 'How do you read it?' "[22] When the expert had read from the law, Jesus' response was, "You have answered correctly."[23] Then He went on to say, "Do this and you will live."[24] When Jesus was at Gethsemane, He told Peter and the two sons of Zebedee, "My soul is overwhelmed with sorrow to the point of death. Stay here and keep watch with me."[25] He states again, "Simply let your 'Yes' be 'Yes', and your 'No', 'No'; anything beyond this comes from the evil one."[26] A person needs to learn to say what he means and mean what he says.

4. *Sharing truth honestly.* It is difficult to be intellectually honest at times, but emotional honesty is far more difficult than intellectual honesty. Paul said, "I speak the truth in Christ — I am not lying, my conscience confirms it in the Holy Spirit — I have great sorrow and unceasing anguish in my heart."[27]

One of the reasons why it is difficult to be emotionally honest is that the heart itself is difficult to know and is deceitful at times. Solomon said:

> The purposes of a man's heart are deep waters, but a man of understanding draws them out.[28]
>
> Many are the plans in a man's heart, but it is the Lord's purpose that prevails.[29]

Jeremiah stated, "The heart is deceitful above all things and beyond cure. Who can understand it?"[30]

5. *Sharing truth in gentleness, with respect, and a clear conscience.* Paul said, "Don't be conceited."[31] Peter stated:

> Always be prepared to give an answer to everyone who asks you to give the reason for the hope that you have. But do this with gentleness and respect, keeping a clear conscience, so that those who speak maliciously against your good behavior in Christ may be ashamed of their slander.[32]

Even if what one says is the truth, if it is spoken harshly, disrespectfully and leaves one feeling guilty and not pleased with his interaction, what truth there might have been frees neither the sharer nor the recipient because it was contaminated in the process. Therefore, spirituality is in part based on sharing the truth in gentleness, meekness and out of a clear conscience.

6. *Sharing truth with grace and salt.* Paul said, "Let your conversation be always full of grace, seasoned with salt, so that you may know how to answer everyone."[33] A sharer is certainly not doing this if his speech (verbally and nonverbally) is to hurt, scorn, humiliate or ridicule the recipient. It is never right to dehumanize another individual. On the other hand, what a sharer says should be filled with grace, or favor, toward the intended recipient, as well as have some preserving qualities which are of substance.

7. *Sharing truth out of one's own spirituality.* Areas in which an individual is not spiritual should not be the areas in which he attempts to assist another individual who is trapped. To illustrate, an individual who is not himself spiritual in sexual areas should not be attempting to restore a brother who is trapped in the sexual area. An individual who is not spiritual in dealing with anger should not be trying to restore a person who is trapped in his anger. This is not to say that there should not be training and close supervision in helping an individual grow spiritually in these and other areas, but is to say that an individual cannot help another become spiritual in an area wherein he is very weak or deplete. Paul expressed it this way:

> Brothers, if someone is caught in some sin, you who are spiritual should restore him gently. But watch yourself, or you also may be tempted. Carry each other's burdens, and in this way you will fulfill the law of Christ. If anyone thinks he is something when he is nothing, he deceives himself. Each man should test his own actions. Then he can take pride in himself, without comparing himself to somebody else, for each one should carry his own load[34]

8. *Looking to see and listening to understand with one's heart.* Although percentagewise it is very seldom mentioned (and stressed even less), listening is one of the most effective ways of increasing an individual's spirituality. A person needs to learn how to listen to

God, to others and to himself. An individual cannot change that of which he is not aware. He cannot become aware until he is willing to listen to God, others and his own feelings, thoughts, and actions. He who would be spiritual must be truly willing to look with his eyes, listen with his ears and understand with his heart what God and others are saying to him, as well as what is going on in his heart and how it is being manifested in his behavior. Solomon said, "I applied my heart to what I observed and learned a lesson from what I saw,"³⁵ Jesus said:

> Though seeing, they do not see; though hearing, they do not hear or under-
> stand. In them is fulfilled the prophecy of Isaiah: "You will be ever hearing but
> never understanding; you will be ever seeing but never perceiving. For this
> people's heart has become calloused; they hardly hear with their ears, and they
> have closed their eyes. Otherwise they might see with their eyes, hear with
> their ears, understand with their hearts and turn, and I would heal them."³⁶

9. *One way for a person to increase both his quality and quantity of spirituality is to increase and deepen his fellowship.* Since fellowship means joint participation in or sharing, a person can deepen and broaden his spiritual growth through different fellowship experiences. *One effective fellowship experience can be a Christian counseling relationship.* It is in this relationship that he can learn something of the meaning of such theological words as faith, hope, love, sin, forgiveness, reconciliation, redemption and mercy.

Paul recognized the holiness of relationships as well as potential dangers in them. He makes this clear in writing to the Corinthians:

> Now this is our boast: Our conscience testifies that we have conducted
> ourselves in the world, and especially in our relationships with you, in the
> holiness and sincerity that are from God.³⁷

> I call God as my witness that it was in order to spare you that I did not return to
> Corinth. Not that we lord it over your faith, but we work with you for your joy,
> because it is by faith you stand firm. So I made up my mind that I would not
> make another painful visit to you. For if I grieve you, who is left to make me
> glad but you whom I have grieved? I wrote as I did so that when I came I
> should not be distressed by those who ought to make me rejoice. I had con-
> fidence in all of you, that you would all share my joy. For I wrote you out of
> great distress and anguish of heart and with many tears, not to grieve you but
> to let you know the depth of my love for you. ³⁸

> You yourselves are our letter, written on our hearts, known and read by
> everybody. You show that you are a letter from Christ, the result of our
> ministry, written not with ink but with the Spirit of the living God, not on
> tablets of stone but on tablets of human hearts.³⁹

Make room for us in your hearts. We have wronged no one, we have corrupted no one, we have exploited no one. I do not say this to condemn you; I have said before that you have such a place in our hearts that we would live or die with you. I am greatly encouraged; in all our troubles my joy knows no bounds. [40]

Counseling is also a relationship through which a client can receive Christ at a different and deeper level. Jesus said, "He who receives you receives me, and he who receives me receives the one who sent me."[41]

Individuals are brought to Christ; they mature in Him through their response to and involvement with at least one other Christian. Depending on the counselor's depth of spirituality, the counselee's motives, and the length and type of relationship they establish, counseling can be a deeply spiritual experience.

One of the serious problems in evangelism is Christians have tried to get persons related to Christ without first getting the individuals related to them; that is, without first establishing an interpersonal relationship. Christians not only tend to try to convert others without an interpersonal relationship, they tend to think that once a person has become a Christian, he can mature without being personally related and intimately involved with others. It should be clearly understood that individuals need far more than attending the *services of the church* and *basket dinners.*

Practically anyone who has been in the church for any length of time is quite familiar with the fact that many individuals are *dropped* after their baptism or restoration. Christians spend much energy in trying to convert nonbelievers and those who have fallen away. Percentagewise, though, little energy is expended in critical, detailed analysis of what is needed in terms of training personnel to teach others creatively how to have ongoing, dynamic and maturing, spiritual relationships. Paul said, "Therefore encourage one another and build each other up, just as in fact you are doing."[42] The early Christians "devoted themselves to the apostles teaching and to the fellowship, to the breaking of bread and to prayer . . . . All the believers were together and had everything in common. Selling their possessions and goods, they gave to anyone as he had need."[43]

COUNSELING – A MEANS TO SPIRITUAL GROWTH

Christian counseling can be a means for individuals to grow spiritually; but not everything called *Christian counseling* is such and some of what is, is mediocre.

Counseling can be an effective method in teaching a person how to be spiritual and how to share his spirituality. One of the concerns which

134

leaders have, and rightly so, is whether or not counseling is spiritual. I am convinced that genuine Christian counseling not only is spiritual, but it can teach a person how to deepen his spirituality as well as share it. Of course, sharing one's spirituality is a means of becoming more spiritual.

FOOTNOTES

[1]Genesis 2:7.
[2]John 4:23, 24.
[3]Romans 12:1.
[4]Isaiah 29:13; Matthew 15:18.
[5]Colossians 3:23.
[6]John 14:6.
[7]John 8:31, 32, 36.
[8]Proverbs 24:32.
[9]Proverbs 14:15.
[10]1 Timothy 4:2.
[11]Ecclesiastes 3:4.
[12]John 4:22.
[13]Ephesians 4:15.
[14]2 Timothy 3:7.
[15]Proverbs 20:15.
[16]Psalms 51:6.
[17]Romans 12:9; 1 Peter 1:22; 1 Corinthians 13:4.
[18]Proverbs 19:11.
[19]Proverbs 25:15.
[20]1 Peter 1:22, 23.
[21]John 4:26.
[22]Luke 10:26.
[23]Luke 10:28.
[24]*Ibid.*
[25]Matthew 26:38.
[26]Matthew 5:37.
[27]Romans 9:1, 2.
[28]Proverbs 20:5.
[29]Proverbs 19:21.
[30]Jeremiah 17:9.
[31]Romans 12:16.
[32]1 Peter 3:15, 16.
[33]Colossians 4:6.

[34]Galatians 6:1-5.
[35]Proverbs 24:32.
[36]Matthew 13:13-15. (See also Isaiah 6:9, 10.)
[37]2 Corinthians 1:12.
[38]2 Corinthians 1:23,24; 2:1-4.
[39]2 Corinthians 3:2-3.
[40]2 Corinthians 7:2-4.
[41]Matthew 10:40.
[42]1 Thessalonians 5:11.
[43]Acts 2:42, 44-45.

Chapter 10
APPROPRIATE SELF-DISCLOSURE – A DYNAMIC COUNSELING PRINCIPLE

A COUNSELOR SHOULD BE AN APPROPRIATE MODEL

In addition to knowing himself, a leader needs to be aware of his transparency or lack of it in his relationships. This is especially true in his counseling. Transparency is a dynamic leadership quality and as a powerful force it has certain dangers. However, these dangers do not warrant a leader's hiding himself from his followers. Leaders are to be examples to their followers, not lords over them. [1] How can they seek to hide themselves from their followers?

Paul said, "Follow my example, as I follow the example of Christ."[2] The New Testament clearly teaches that both Christ and Paul revealed themselves to their followers discreetly. Christians would be wise to follow the examples of Christ and Paul in appropriately disclosing themselves to their followers.

WHAT IS INAPPROPRIATE MODELING?

An analytical thinker naturally raises the question, "What is or is not appropriate self-disclosure?" I think seven ways of inappropriately disclosing oneself are:

1. Monopolizing other people's time bragging about one's accomplishments and how great he and/or his family are.

2. Being boastful, arrogant, haughty and sarcastic to keep distance in the relationship and avoid sharing one's true self.

3. Indiscreetly sharing his feelings, thoughts, and behavior. A person should not share areas of himself about which he does not have a concrete basis for believing another individual would accept what he shares.

4. Sharing one's self (thoughts, feelings, behaviors) without a basis of trust and respect.

5. Sharing out of compulsion, guilt or shame. A counselor may share some guilt or shame, but his sharing should not be primarily motivated by these feelings.

6. Sharing in order to manipulate some individuals while at the same time avoiding others.

7. Attempting to get others to feel sorry for, take care of, or excuse him for what he is doing or has done.

WHAT DOES APPROPRIATE SELF-DISCLOSURE MEAN?

Appropriate self-disclosure is built on and grows out of openness, honesty, concern, respect, and responsibility. Appropriate self-disclosure is not only scriptural and healthy for a leader, but necessary for depth discovery and profound faith. Leaders who reveal themselves in interrelating with their followers will discover their followers will tend to be open to revealing themselves for discovery and growth.

SEVEN AREAS OF SELF-DISCLOSURE

There are at least seven areas in which a leader (whether formal teaching or counseling) can be helpful to another in his growth process if he discriminately shares himself. Although they are considered separately, these areas of self-disclosure are interwoven.

1. *Revealing one's humanness.* Individuals have shared with me through the years that they did not feel their leaders were human; that is, they did not see them as struggling, or having struggled, with the basic questions and problems of life. (Granted, their perception may have been inaccurate.) They have seen their leaders come across as though they were naive about life itself — not having any personal, marital, family or vocational struggles. There was no differentiation in the blacks, the whites, and grays of life. They put all matters in an *either/or* context while the individuals themselves were struggling with the *both/and* context. It is true that there are rights and wrongs which are absolute, however, in everyday life most of people's struggles are in the gray area. It is hard to determine the black and white because they are so intermingled. If a person is going to confront most of the issues with which he is involved in a manner which will enable him to resolve them, he must be able to hold in tension the good and the bad which is inherent in the issue he is confronting.

138

It should be understood that many of the struggles in human relations in the family or church deal with the complexities of human beings, whether or not they are involved with one another. This puts enormous pressure on those concerned. There is also an area in which individuals struggle with their lives, or try to avoid struggling, which they perceive as wrong or right; but really it is neither. Many people suffer considerable stress because they are embarrassed about the way their bodies are shaped or not shaped, where they grew up, the school they attended or did not attend, the fact that they ask questions about the teachings and practices of a congregation. The list goes on and on, but none of these are sinful. One of the reasons for such misconception is the lack of appropriate modeling or self-disclosure of the leaders with whom individuals are identified.

2. *Revealing one's fear.* It seems that for centuries it has been difficult for man to knowledge his fear. The one-talent man was even dishonest at first to keep from acknowledging his fear.[3] On the other hand, it seems that Paul had very little difficulty in acknowledging his fear. Notice what he said: "For when we came into Macedonia, this body of ours had no rest, but we were harrassed at every turn − conflicts on the outside, fears within."[4] It has been established time and time again that fear ignored will only turn into a phobia, but a fear recognized, analyzed, faced and worked through ceases to be.

Related to fear is the word *anxiety*. Fear is usually easy to recognize because so often it relates to something concrete of which an individual is aware. On the other hand, anxiety may be made up of a conglomerate of fears. It is that overwhelming feeling which an individual experiences when he feels that he or a value of his is threatened. He may or may not know about what he is anxious. Anxiety, like fear, must be analyzed and worked through before it will really cease. Anxiety can be viewed as healthy for a person if he accepts, analyzes, faces and works through it.

Often the following passage is cited to prove that a Christian should never be anxious. Notice! "Do not be anxious about anything, but in everything, by prayer and petition, with thanksgiving, present your requests to God."[5] By the time a person has done what Paul stated in this verse, he has worked through his anxiety. An individual is no longer anxious when he can reduce his anxiety to specifics and *in everything* or in every specific he can pray and petition to God and work to the point where he can even feel some gratitude. Contrary to what some have thought, Paul really gives the formula for confronting anxiety in a healthy manner rather than pretending one does not have anxiety or should not have it.

Anxiety, when properly understood and responded to, is healthy for a person rather than sinful. Through years of hard work in overcoming my own fear of anxiety, as well as some false teaching about it, I have come to see that anxiety is to a person as temperature is to his body. Anxiety gives one an immediate reading when he feels he or a value he holds is threatened. When a medical doctor discovers a person has a fever, he is aware that infection is somewhere in the patient's body and responds accordingly. When an informed individual discovers he is anxious, he is aware that his person or a value he holds feel threatened. Instead of trying to ignore his anxiety, he analyzes it − expecting to determine the cause(s) and work through it. Although the causes of anxiety may be unrealistic, the feeling-effects on a person are the same as if the causes for his anxiety were real.

3. *Revealing one's pain.* Pain *per se* is neither good nor bad, but is inherent in being human as well as in one's growth process. If leaders are to be of real value in helping their followers grow, they, of necessity, must help them learn how to deal with their pain or hurts in the process of growth itself.[6] There are leaders who communicate to their followers (whether intentionally or otherwise) that pain should be overlooked, ignored, or avoided and not faced up to, analyzed and worked through. I am of the opinion that a person can face and deal with his pain easier than he can run from it and/or deal with a lie. Stein says, "The disturbing truth is more important to health than the comfortable lie."[7] Of course, an individual can have accumulated so much pain that he cannot deal with all of it at once. The nature, intensity, amount of buildup, ego strength and coping skills determine how much, with whom, and for how long an individual should focus on his pain at a given time.

Society today places much stress on pleasure, instant gratification and the absence of pain. This influence has caused many to feel there is something wrong with them if they are hurting or have to postpone gratifying a desire or deny its gratification altogether. The *instant society* in which Americans live has also influenced leaders in the church to the point that some of them seem to feel it is natural to expect instant growth. Even worse than this is the idea that growth can take place without struggle and facing one's pain. Certainly I am not suggesting that leaders attempt to create pain by rigidity,

140

authoritarianism and harshness, but I am firmly persuaded that pain is inherent in being human and in the growth process of an individual.

Perhaps it would be relatively easy for a reader to agree intellectually that pain is inherent in being human and growing as an individual. But, I am relatively sure it would be difficult for a reader to accept such on an emotional level. I know it is difficult for me at times when I am working with a person who is experiencing his pain; sometimes I find myself backing off because it does hurt to help a person grow. Although helping an individual to face and work through his pain is not easy, it is necessary if he is to grow in the area in which he is experiencing pain.

One serious problem which a leader may have when he begins to look at and help a follower deal with his pain in a therapeutic sense is this puts the leader in touch with his own pain, which he may have avoided in a particular area. Another serious problem results when a leader gets lost in his own pain and confuses his pain with that of his follower.

To the extent that a leader has not run from, but has honestly faced and worked through his own pain, to that extent he will desire both consciously and unconsciously to help a follower face and work through his pain. A painful experience has been worked through when an individual can recall its components and be open to them, but he does not feel pain through such recall.

4. *Revealing one's suffering.* Paul was very precise in sharing that he was suffering. Notice what he says: "That is why I am suffering as I am."[8] He also said, "That is why, for Christ's sake, I delight in weaknesses, in insults, in hardships, in persecutions, in difficulties. For when I am weak, then I am strong."[9]

Paul's sufferings, as well as disclosing he was suffering were not embarrassing for him. He was not ashamed of disclosing his suffering because he knew whom he had believed. At the time Paul wrote the above passages he had a number of years experience during which he was involved with Christ and His way of life. Therefore, one can safely assume he had internalized many of the concepts which he verbally proclaimed. Through his internalization he was growing in trust, or faith, and was able to say that he knew Him in Whom he believed. Notice! "Yet I am not ashamed, because I know Whom I have believed, and am convinced that He is able to guard what I have entrusted to Him for that day."[10]

141

One of the bases for self-disclosure is when an individual reveals himself to another on the basis of trust. However, trust cannot develop without an individual's confronting his doubts and questions in the relationship. He must then expose himself to others as well as be exposed to himself in the process of working through these doubts and questions. Given enough time, a person can become relatively comfortable in disclosing more and more of himself. This can be accomplished if, without rejection and humiliation, he is able to work successfully through his doubts and questions about who he is, what he believes, where and with whom he fits, in what areas and to what depths. Disclosure without trust is dangerous and can be very hurtful. On the other hand, a leader who is too ashamed to genuinely acknowledge his weaknesses and suffering when appropriate will never be a strong leader, but will tend to perpetuate weakness and sickness in himself and his followers. Thus, it becomes very important for an individual to develop trust in a relationship. Then, when he reveals himself he can know assuredly, based on past experiences, that the person will receive him and not make light of, put down or humiliate him.

Paul stated he not only knew the One in Whom he believed, but he was convinced He was able to guard what he had entrusted to Him until that day. It is important to know the person in whom one believes, but it is also important for one to be thoroughly convinced, based on experience, that the individual can guard or keep what is shared with him. One of the fears so many in the church feel is they cannot and/or will not keep what is shared. One's disclosing himself, which is actually giving a part of himself, should be treated sacred and holy and a basis of confidentiality should be established.

Since troubles are painful and frightening, leaders tend to avoid looking at trouble, much less helping another deal with his troubles. Paul pointed out to the Philippians, "It was good of you to share in my troubles."[11] That being the case, a Christian's participating in helping another to deal constructively and creatively with his troubles can potentially be helpful to that person.

5. *Revealing one's shame.* Shame, humiliation, ridicule, embarrassment, etc., are feelings an individual experiences when he is exposed to himself and/or to others when he does not want such exposure. It is so private that no one else can experience, but the embarrassed person feels the *whole world* can perceive him with the same precision and clarity with which he sees himself. In reality, another individual can, at best, only see that he is embarrassed, but can never

142

experience the specific dynamics, even if the embarrassed person shares them.

An individual becomes ashamed essentially because of two reasons. In growing up he learned to think, feel and relate to himself and others in a particular way and when he changes environment and relates to individuals of a different background (if he wishes to impress them and/or if they are important to him) the particualr differences will likely be embarrassing to him. This is especially true if what he was taught, how he related, and/or was related to, in his family was perceived by him as being the only right or appropriate way to relate or act. A second reason why a person may become ashamed is through verbal and/or nonverbal expression he reveals and/or exposes himself in areas wherein he does not want to be disclosed either to himself or to others.

The focus of shame is on the self. When one is embarrassed it is easy for him to interpret his feeling of humiliation and ridicule as meaning that he is a ridiculous, stupid, or weird person. Early in life (before age two with some individuals) a person begins experiencing either his total self or parts of himself and certain behaviors as shameful. Very early he begins developing feelings of a negative nature, such as bad, dirty and nasty. Since the nature of shame is to hide or cover to keep from being exposed, most individuals begin very early in life the process of avoiding looking at themselves and allowing others to see them because they, their thoughts, feelings and behaviors are seen by them as being shameful. Most shameful experiences originated in a person's youth. Since shame tends to overwhelm a person (especially a child) and the nature of it is to hide from the exposure because of a lack of correct and adequate knowledge and experience, a person becomes shameful about many thoughts, feelings and behaviors which are natural and normal. The longer a person goes without being appropriately exposed to himself, his thoughts, feelings and behaviors in a sincere, caring and nonhumiliating manner, the less of a person or himself he can become. It stands to reason the more of self that is hidden from oneself, his teachers, parents, etc., the less of the self is being developed.

Scores of individuals whom I have seen needed to come to therapy not because of their being bad, dirty or nasty, but because of the prolonged shame of normal and natural feelings, thoughts and behaviors. Their humiliation not only kept them from growing, but contributed to much of their misery. Being ashamed made them unhappy as well as unfulfilled.

Since most church programs and Bible lessons are developed out of the guilt instead of the shame dynamic, Christians tend to get very little help in overcoming their shame. Much of the focus in Christian education has been on *doing* or *not doing* certain things. Many of my clients have told me their leaders gave them the impression they were to obey without question and not expect answers to their questions or understand the reason for doing what was requested. It is true that Christians are to do what the Word teaches;[12] however, if one is only a *doer,* he may be simply a hollow, bitter, sarcastic or arrogant reactor rather than a maturing Christ-like individual. He may be able to quote Scriptures, sound deeply spiritual and honor God with his lips, but his heart may be far from God.[13]

Paul needs to be taken seriously when he said, "Whatever you do, work at it with all your heart, as working for the Lord, not for men."[14] However, just doing what God says is not enough. Paul also said, "For in Christ Jesus neither circumcision nor uncircumcision has any value. The only thing that counts is faith expressing itself through love."[15] He further stated: "The goal of this command is love, which comes from a pure heart, a good concience and a sincere faith."[16]

The Bible is not just a simple list of *do's* and *don'ts;* it is really a mirror of the soul. In other words, the Bible exposes man to himself. Unless a person sees himself as he is in reality and gets at least a glimpse of what he is capable of becoming, he actually has not seen himself. Notice what both James and the Hebrews writer said:

> Do not merely listen to the word, and so deceive yourselves. Do what it says. Anyone who listens to the word but does not do what it says is like a man who looks at his face in a mirror and, after looking at himself, goes away and immediately forgets what he looks like. But the man who looks intently into the perfect law that gives freedom, and continues to do this, not forgetting what he has heard, but doing it – he will be blessed in what he does.[17]
>
> The word of God is living and active. Sharper than any double-edged sword, it penetrates even to the dividing soul and spirit, joints and marrow; it judges the thoughts and attitudes of the heart.[18]

Doing (even what is right) can be a means for a person to avoid looking at himself. Most of the individuals I know seem to study the Bible to prove either what they are doing is right or what others are doing is wrong.

One of the serious dangers of a *doer* is that he may never integrate his behaviors, thoughts and feelings. In other words, he may never see meaning in what he does. A Christian can integrate his feelings, thoughts and behaviors only to the extent that his Christianity has meaning and purpose to him.

A *doer* may outwardly appear to be very active but inwardly feel frustrated, lonely, empty and anxious because he is neither going anywhere in particular nor accomplishing anything specifically. Even though a *doer* may finish a task, he may be relieved because it is over or frustrated because he has run out of something to do. The person who is in the process of learning to integrate his behavior, thoughts and emotions completes a task and feels a sense of accomplishment, satisfaction, joy and peace.

If the above is accurate, there is validity in taking seriously the concept that Christian leaders should not guide their followers into behavior as such, but lead them into looking into themselves openly, honestly, respectfully, responsibly, caringly, tenderly and perserveringly. Leaders will be successful in this approach largely to the degree that they reveal themselves openly and honestly to their followers in the leading-following or teaching-learning process. Leaders can best get their followers to look at and deal with their shameful thoughts, feelings and behaviors if they will first discreetly disclose their own shameful thoughts, feelings and behaviors. They need to be aware of and skillfully utilize the different levels of learning.

The *awareness level* of learning has reference to a person who is familiar with particular phrases and expressions. When he hears a particular sermon or lesson, he is simply aware that he has heard it before.

The *memory level* of learning has reference to memorization of dates, places, persons and verses without understanding the meanings of words, sentence structure and both the immediate and general context.

The *insight level* of learning refers to a person knowing the meanings of words, sentence structure in a particular passage, how these interrelate to each other and how they are used in other passages as well as understanding the immediate and general context in which they appear. Naturally, upon hearing something familiar, a person can be aware of and even memorize dates, persons, places and verses without really having any insight into what the writer is attempting to communicate.

The *assimilation level* of learning is digesting or applying the lesson to the extent and long enough to where what is being learned becomes a part of the person himself.

One of the ways leaders and their followers avoid revealing themselves is through talking in the second and third persons. My experience as a minister and therapist reveals it is next to impossible for individuals to reveal themselves through talking in the second or third person. Many lectures, sermons and Bible classes are presented almost exclusively in the second or third person. Most Christians I know talk in terms of *you, he, they,* and *them* instead of *I, me,* and *my.* Self-disclosure forces a person to share his behavior, thoughts and feelings by saying, "I believe . . . ", "I feel . . . ", and "I think . . . "

Another method a leader uses to refrain from disclosing himself is through applying Scripture to other persons or groups (likely to prove them unacceptable). Application or assimiliation of biblical knowledge is far more difficult and painful than intellectually learning biblical facts and concepts and has received less attention historically. In addition, when application is made, it tends to be vague, general and/or applied to another person or group. Many of my clients have said their leaders came across as though they were perfect.

A leader who is cold, authoritarian, guarded, rigid, and decisive is neither disclosing his shameful thoughts, feelings and behavior nor is he modeling specifically and clearly how to accept one's self, deal with one's shame and feel clean and lovable instead of feeling humiliated.

A leader who laughs at, puts down and humiliates others neither overcomes his own humiliation nor effectively models the beauty and goodness of self-acceptance. A leader who does not demonstrate from his own personal experiences and attitudes that he has tasted and discovered "that the Lord is good"[19] will likely never convince his followers that Christianity can be an "inexpressable and glorious joy."[20]

Both David and Jesus recognized it is possible for a person to be ashamed of whom he believes as well as what he believes. David struggled with this as seen in his expression, "In you I trust, Oh my God. Do not let me be put to shame, nor let my enemies triumph over me."[21] Jesus spoke to this issue when He said, "If anyone is ashamed of me and my words in this adulterous and sinful generation, the Son of Man will be ashamed of him when he comes in his Father's glory with the holy angels."[22] David had put his trust in God, but apparently he had not had the time or the experience of living for God to overcome his fear of embarrassment. Paul was able to say, "I know whom I have believed;"[23] thus, since he knew and had become convinced of whom as well as what he believed, he was not ashamed. Jesus recognized it was possible for a person to be ashamed of him as well as his teachings in the presence of those who were sinful. The Bible teaches that ministers and Christian leaders need to be sensitive to helping their students become very knowledgeable not only in God or Christ, but in what they believe as well. One of things that help people drift away from the church is their embarrassment which is never looked at in an intelligent manner. Sometimes leaders oversimplify the problem of development in the church. When an individual comes to them with questions which are embarrassing to reveal he should not be humiliated, put down or given a simplistic answer. He should be helped to see himself, God and the Word in a deeper manner. This can enable him to look at whom and what he believes and discover that there is no need to be ashamed.

David had his problems with shame and Jesus talked about individuals being ashamed of him and his Word. Just as this was true in times past, it is true today. Christian leaders and their followers do in fact have their problems with shame.

A person may become embarrassed or ashamed of the one in whom he believes or the basis of his belief. For the Christian, this is the Word of God. There are several reasons why this could happen:

a. He may have believed that no one else knew any truth but him and his particular group or congregation. After getting into another educational setting or being exposed to what others believe and teach, he may have discovered that others, too, have some truth. This could be an embarrassing discovery.

b. He may have thought he thoroughly understood a particular doctrine and really knew essentially all truth, but in college or with other informed individuals may have received questions, etc., which exposed his ignorance. Such exposure could be embarrassing.

c. He may have thought his view of truth was comprehensive and exhaustive. He may have later discovered that his knowledge was shallow and limited and some of what he thought he knew did not really correspond scripturally or otherwise to reality. He may have been afraid and/or embarrassed to look at what he claimed to know under the criticism of someone else for fear that he may again be exposed nakedly to himself and others.

147

d. He may have discovered that he accepted and taught certain things as a means of hiding from himself and others instead of being open and transparent.

Paul was psychologically accurate when he precisely stated why he was not ashamed of whom and what he believed. "I know whom I have believed, and am convinced that he is able to guard what I have entrusted to him for that day."[24]

A person can believe and share his beliefs without being embarrassed if:

a. He precisely *knows why* he believes *what* he does.

b. He has become *convinced* that the individual with whom he is sharing is able to guard what he is sharing or entrusting to him.

6. *Revealing one's needs.* Paul said: "Therefore I urge you to imitate me."[25] Again, he states: "Follow my example, as I follow the example of Christ."[26] He also exhorts that "whatever you have learned or received or heard from me, or seen in me – put into practice. And the God of peace will be with you."[27]

A leader should grow to the point that he is not ashamed to share with his followers not only that he has needs, but also what his specific needs are at a given time. Paul was a clear example in acknowledging what he needed from various individuals. He could ask individuals to visit him, acknowledge that certain ones were helpful to him in his ministry, and request that his cloak, scrolls and parchments be brought to him.[28] He could specifically ask for a place in Christians' hearts.[29] Although he pleaded with the Lord for what he wanted, he could accept the fact that not all of his requests would be granted.[30]

One of the problems which some religious leaders have is they are too ashamed to acknowledge their needs to themselves, much less to their followers. Through such lack of acknowledgement, they continue trying to cover their humiliation, but they end up cheating themselves and their followers. Paul was able to share he had been in need at times and he also knew what it was like to have plenty. Individuals sometimes share with me their leaders leave the impression they are ashamed to acknowledge they need help which perhaps their followers could give them. Often when a leader does acknowledge a need, it is generalized and so vaguely stated that people (followers) do not really know what the leader's needs are. Some leaders tend to feel that needing help from someone else is something of which to be ashamed. Paul said, "I can do everything through him who gives me strength,"[31] but he did not mean that he never had needs which others could meet or that he did not make specific requests for certain needs to be met by his brethren.

7. *Revealing one's conflict.* Conflict is inherent in being human. It is present within one's self, marriage, family and other interpersonal relationships. The prevailing idealized view of the normal person, marriage and family is that he or they are free from stress or conflict. This myth is even perpetuated by some leaders. Although it is done more implicitly than explicitly, it is nevertheless kept alive. Paul was very explicit in sharing that he was at times in conflict.

> I do not know what I am doing. For what I want to do I do not do, but what I hate I do.[12]
>
> If I am to go on living in the body, this will mean fruitful labor for me. Yet, what shall I choose? I do not know! I am torn between the two: I desire to depart and be with Christ, which is better by far; but it is more necessary for you that I remain in the body. Convinced of this, I know that I will remain and I will continue with all of you for your progress and joy in the faith.[13]
>
> For when we came into Macedonia, this body of ours had no rest, but we were harassed at every turn – conflicts on the outside, fears within.[14]

Individuals sometimes share with me that their leaders leave the impression that they, their marriages and families are without conflict. Appropriate and discretionary disclosing of a leader's conflicts can be helpful to his followers. It is absurd for a leader to leave the impression with his followers that an individual, couple or family can always live in harmony, cooperate with each other, never get ruffled or experience conflict.

Transparency (or self-disclosure) like any other dynamic leadership quality, should be studied critically because it, too, has dangers involved with it. Even so, the dangers by no means should be the reasons for leaders to ignore disclosing themselves. Neither should they refuse to learn whatever they can from self-disclosure and implement it discreetly themselves. In fact, transparency correctly understood, wisely and persistently practiced by a leader will naturally enable him to be more effective.

FOOTNOTES

[1] 1Peter 5:3.
[2] 1 Corinthians 11:1.
[3] Matthew 25:24, 25.
[4] 2 Corinthians 7:5.
[5] Philippians 4:6.
[6] Obviously a person may experience pain as result of sin.

[7]Edward V. Stein, *The Stranger Inside You* (Philadelphia: Westminster Press, 1965), p. 39.

[8]2 Timothy 1:12.

[9]2 Corinthians 12:10.

[10]2 Timothy 1:12.

[11]Philippians 4:14.

[12]James 1:22.

[13]Matthew 15:8.

[14]Colossians 3:23.

[15]Galatians 5:6.

[16]1 Timothy 1:5.

[17]James 1:22-25.

[18]Hebrews 4:12.

[19]1 Peter 2:3.

[20]1 Peter 1:8.

[21]Psalms 25:2.

[22]Mark 8:38.

[23]2 Timothy 1:12.

[24]*Ibid.*

[25]1 Corinthians 4:16.

[26]1 Corinthians 11:1.

[27]Philippians 4:9.

[28]2 Timothy 4:9-13.

[29]2 Corinthians 7:2.

[30]2 Corinthians 12:7-10.

[31]Philippians 4:13.

[32]Romans 7:15.

[33]Philippians 1:22-25.

[34]2 Corinthians 7:5.

Chapter 11

WHAT IS IN IT FOR ME?

COUNSELOR NEEDS TO KNOW WHAT HE EXPECTS TO GET FROM CLIENT

Solomon said, "The end of a matter is better than its beginning."[1]

This Scripture can be applied to the counseling relationship as well as other areas of life. In order for this to take place, there are certain questions that need specific answers. A counselor needs to find out from his counselee why he came to see him now instead of later, and what he needs or wants from the counselor. Equally important for therapeutic purposes is the need for the counselor to seriously raise and answer the question, "What is in it for me?" This may sound arrogant, selfish, and unchristian to some individuals, but it is basic to effective counseling.

ONE COUNSELS TO MEET A NEED

A person counsels, in part, to meet one or more of his own needs. A counselor should have a clear understanding of his needs, and insight into how to meet them. He also should be involved in a variety of relationships which meets his needs at different levels. The more satisfactorily he is meeting them, the more likely he has a healthy motivation to be involved with a particular client.

An individual has such needs as:

1. To love and be loved.

2. To be involved from infancy in a loving, trusting relationship. This helps him to learn how to love and trust himself, others and God.

3. Freedom, truth and responsibility. A person should be free of the controlling power of fear, guilt, and shame. He needs a realistic, adequate, and precisely-defined value system which is based on truth. Freedom and truth demand that he be responsible. Although I treated these needs separately, functionally they are inseparable.

Responsibility is a comprehensive word which has several inherent components. To be responsible requires a person to be accountable or answerable — he must account to or answer for his thoughts, words, or actions. He answers not only to God and others, but also to himself.

Another aspect of responsibility is option or choice.[2] Regardless of the situation or circumstances, a person always has a choice. It may not be what he likes or prefers, and he may not be aware that he does have an option (many individuals are not). However, if he is open and creatively searches, he will discover he has at least one choice and often there are a number of options in a given situation. One of the major difficulties a person has is really believing he has a choice, but he can enjoy his freedom only to the extent that he chooses wisely.

To be responsible also means a person learns how to think, analyze, have courage to make his own decisions, and accept the consequences without trying to blame someone else. To be responsible also means that one exercises self-discipline or self-control.

The responsible person is one who recognizes, accepts, understands, and respectfully expresses his feelings when it is appropriate. He is fully aware that he is accountable to God, others, and self. He operates with openness, honesty, and respect toward himself, others and God.[3] Since one is neither omniscient nor perfect in making and carrying out his decisions, he sins. At this point, repentance and confession become inherent dynamics of responsibility. Since truth is not inherent in man, it becomes necessary for one to change his mind and correct his behavior. He needs to make appropriate apologies in order to acquire a deep and continual sense of belonging. This leads to appropriate and adequate self-esteem — neither thinking too little or too much of self. Paul said,

> For by the grace given to me I say to every one of you: Do not think of yourself more highly than you ought, but rather think of yourself with sober judgment, in accordance with the measure of faith God has given you.[4]

WHAT MADE ME THINK I COULD HELP PEOPLE?

It is important to know what causes individuals to get divorces, abuse or abandon their children, leave a particular ministry, or quit the church. One way of gaining more insight is by obtaining a clearer perception of why they enter intrapersonal and interpersonal relationships. It should be understood that the following reasons overlap and are interwoven and one or more will usually stand out as being the essential reasons a particular person entered a religious ministry, got married, and/or became a parent. Of course, the reason will vary from person to person. The following are some reasons why individuals enter into an intrapersonal and interpersonal relationship:

1. *Searching for love,*[5] having never really experienced genuine human love over a long period of time in adequate amounts.

2. *Seeking to find a good parent.* I have seen, and see, people searching for their father and/or mother. In an attempt to find them (psychologically), they enter into some religious ministry, get married, and /or have children.[6]

3. *Reaction to an early death and/or abandonment by a parental figure.*[7]

4. *Need to dominate or possess others.* [8]

5. *Fear of giving way to the temptation of impurity.*[9]

6. *Being paranoid, feeling called of God to set the world or church right on some issues.*[10] While I have seen this more frequently as a reason for entering a religious ministry, this is a reason why a few people whom I have seen have gotten married and/or had children.

7. *Having guilt feelings.*[11]

8. *Thinking it an opportunity to advance financially, socially, and psychologically.*

9. *Desiring to be the center of attention.*

10. *Believing that they would be looked up to, respected, or even idolized.*[12]

11. *Having a self-fantasy of being a great leader, husband, wife, and/or parent.*[13].

12. *Desiring to wield considerable authority.*

13. *Expecting to receive certain favors and special considerations.*

14. *Believing they could escape some of life's hard experiences.*[14]

15. *Thinking it would be an easy life or make life easier.*

16. *Having had pressure from a parent, preacher, or some other important person.*[14]

17. *Having a sincere and mature love for God, self, and others*[16] with insight into how they could realistically meet their basic needs while at the same time serve God and help others. They saw their decision to enter the relationship or add another person to it (have a child) as a matter of choice, not compulsion. It was an opportunity for growth and development, not just a means to survive or avoid loneliness or hell, etc.

There are at least five basic principles which underlie a person's decision to enter intrapersonal and interpersonal relationships such as religious ministry or marriage.

1. One should realize that every decision is made by a person shaped by this total experiences and relationships. This is true regardless of whether they are adequate or inadequate, healthy or unhealthy.[17]

2. Any decision to enter an intrapersonal and interpersonal relationship, be it vocational or otherwise, expresses the needs, drives, basic patterns, and relationships of the person making the decision. Of course, they exist in each individual in varying intensities and in different degrees of conflict.[18]

3. Due to the American culture, most of the time vocational, marital, and many family decisions are made before a person has achieved a high level of emotional or religious maturity.[19]

4. The very strong, controlling, and determining elements in a decision are often unconscious. The Wise Man said, "The purpose of a man's heart are deep waters, but a man of understanding draws them out."[20] Nevertheless, "it is a trap for a man to dedicate something rashly and only later to consider his vows."[21] Paul said, "I do not know what I am doing. For what I want to do I do not do, but what I hate I do . . . . For what I do is not the good I want to do; no, the evil I do not want to do — this I keep on doing. Now if I do what I do not want to do, it is not I who do it, but it is sin living in me that does it."[22]

Wise correctly states:

It should be remembered that a religious calling offers a great opportunity for delusional self-interpretation of the kind that inflates the ego and feeds pride in other defenses. Sometimes unconscious factors, because of their strong and mysterious nature, are interpreted or misinterpreted as being the direct working of God in human life. A boy may decide to go into the ministry because his mother, or some other person, wants him to, and he may rationalize this as a divine call.[23]

Whitlock says, "It may be helpful to recall that the 'call to the ministry' is not a matter of fact, but is an interpretation of complex human experiences."[24]

There are also unconscious and conscious factors in a person's self-image, which relate directly and indirectly to his decision to enter a particular ministry;[25] for example, "his ideas and feelings about who he is, what kind of person he is, and how others should relate to him."[26] It is clear that one's self-image does not develop without reason,[27] although man tends to see things as *he is* not as *they are*.[28]

A person's conception of himself influences not only his decision to enter a religious ministry, but also his work as a particular type of leader.[29] Wise states:

> A self-fantasy of being a great leader or one of being in a humiliating relationship to others will lead to different kinds of ministries, and each may be disguised by conscious show of humility and theological rationalizations. A person who feels himself as inferior may be strongly attracted to the mission field because he sees himself as a superior working with inferiors. This is both unhealthy and unchristian, but it has been known to be a larger factor in the 'call to the mission field' which certain individuals have felt.
>
> A deeply dependent person will be deeply dependent in his religious life; in one who is motivated strongly by guilt or hostility or anxiety, these will be prominent. Where an individual is open to new insights and growth is taking place, his religious life will partake and assist in this growth. Where an individual is predominantly defensive in his reactions, he will be defensive against new religious insights and growth, and will also, paradoxically, use religion as a defense against growth.[30]

5. Relationships with parents and other significant adults play a meaningful role, both consciously and unconsciously, in decisions for religious work,[31] getting married, or having children. There are a number of factors involved in a person's making a decision to enter intrapersonal and interpersonal relationships. It takes a detailed analysis of the numerous, complex, conscious and unconscious processes before one can be really knowledgeable about why he entered a particular ministry, got married, or had children.

DISILLUSIONMENT, A FACT OF LIFE

The word *burnout* came into professional literature in 1974,[32] but the dynamic components of this expression have been around for ages. Burnout, or disillusionment, is a fact of life. Everyone gets disillusioned as a helping person, spouse, or parent. The more immature and unrealistically motivated a person was to enter a particular ministry or relationship, the less he has matured in these roles and the more intense and comprehensive his disillusionment will become. Burnout is contagious. It can easily spread to every area of one's life.

BURNOUT IS RELATED TO NEEDS

Burnout is related to the degree to which one meets his personal, marital, parental, professional, and other social needs in a balanced and satisfactory manner. It should be understood that a person's

155

needs are circular in nature. Once a need is met, that condition temporarily subsides. For example, an individual gets hungry, he eats, and is filled; but given a few hours he is hungry again. A child needs tender loving care. He comes to mother and gets his need for affection met. He then goes and plays by himself or with others for a while and then returns to his mother for more attention.

Once a particular need is met, the means of meeting it are no longer pleasurable and if continued will make the person reject what was enjoyable and satisfying to him a short time before. This is equally true of both physical and emotional needs. A person can get just as sick of too much hugging and kissing as he can too much ice cream. A person should have his needs met in a variety of ways at different times on different levels. If one attempts to meet a particular need the same way and on the same level each time it cycles, after a period of time that method will be resisted because of its lack of satisfaction. An individual has a number of personal, marital, parental, professional, and other social needs that are interwoven and do overlap.

When one is trying to get a need met, he may behave in a way that is opposite of what he is wanting or needs. A person may need affection but sulk or pout. An individual who needs to feel care and concern may say and act as though he does not. A person may say he does not care but may actually be hurting because he needs others to care. He is unable to get it through certain means and on the level in which he needs it. It is easy for a person to be confused and not know that he is acting in ways that are opposite from what he needs. He may know this, but because of his shame and anxiety, continue his inappropriate behavior. This behavior is not only characteristic of children, but also of adults.

A person may neglect different areas of needs as he tries to meet them in a given area. On certain levels some needs are easier to meet and can be met quicker than others. One needs to alternate meeting his needs on different levels between personal, marital, parental, professional, and other social relationships. It is not wise for a person to stop or *get stuck* in any one area. This is not to say that one area may not need more attention at a given time than others.

One danger is getting *lost* in a given area and remaining there for a long period of time. A real danger occurs when an individual gets lost and is not even aware of it. When and if one gets lost, whether he is aware or not, a number of costly mistakes can easily be made.

For example, a person may leave a particular ministry abruptly and without thought. He may end his marriage, neglect his children, or become cynical, abusive, and dehumanizing in a number of different passive or aggressive ways. Therefore, balance in meeting one's needs in different areas on various levels should be highly sought by an individual.

Each need has various levels. For example, the need for affection. It may be met through a wink, a smile or a brief touch (pat on the shoulder, quick hug or firm grip of the hand, etc). On another occasion, it may require considerable verbal and nonverbal communication for it to be met satisfactorily.

ENTHUSIASM, THE FIRST STAGE OF DISILLUSIONMENT

Enthusiasm is a powerful word. It is necessary for a person to be properly motivated himself, as well as motivate others. It is *dangerous* when he gets caught up in his own enthusiasm and what seems right to him, because he *may ignore reason, reality and refuse to listen to advice.* Solomon said:

> A simple man believes anything, but a prudent man gives thought to his steps.[33]
> There is a way that seems right to a man, but in the end it leads to death.[34]
> All a man's ways seem innocent to him, but motives are weighed by the Lord.[35]
> Listen to advice and accept instruction, and in the end you will be wise.[37]
> Stop listening to instruction, my son, and you will stray from the words of knowledge.[38]

It is easy for the enthusiastic person to get caught up in his pride or arrogance. It is important for one to consider seriously what Solomon had to say about the arrogant side of pride. He stated:

> Pride goes before destruction, a haughty spirit before a fall.[39]
> Pride only breeds quarrels, but wisdom is found in those who take advice.[40]
> When pride comes, then comes disgrace, but with humility comes wisdom.[41]
> Before his downfall a man's heart is proud, but humility comes before honor.[42]

ENTHUSIASM IS DESIRABLE ALTHOUGH THERE ARE DANGERS INVOLVED

Enthusiam can make a person's work more enjoyable, less strenuous and will be beneficial to him to the degree that:

1. It grows out of who he really is and what he actually wants to do because he has clear insight into how such would meet his particular need.

2. It grows out of insight into how a particular behavior meets a specific need at a given level and how this interrelates to his other needs.

3. It grows out of the joy and satisfaction which comes from meeting a particular need instead of *psyching oneself up* because needs in other areas have not been met. A person may *act excited* in a given relationship at a particular time to avoid feeling the pain he is having as a result of a need not being met satisfactorily in his marriage or other relationships. When family relationships are strained, it may be easier to be warmly related to another individual(s) than to confront the problems at home. A Bible teacher may enjoy relating to her students more than she does to her own children. It may be more exciting to *visit the sick* than to help a sick spouse or child.

Sometimes it becomes very difficult to know how to get one's needs met on the level which he desires. It requires considerable courage and patience. Thus, it becomes very tempting for one to turn his attention to relationships in which he can get some of his needs met with less frustration and effort. When this happens, it gets easier and more tempting for him to narrow his focus and withdraw more from his relationships in which he is experiencing difficulty. After a while, he begins to become frustrated because other needs he has (even in that relationship) are not being met satisfactoriy. Even the ones that are being met may not be on the desired levels.

Enthusiasm about an area of one's life does not carry over into other areas if there is a significant buildup of pain and hostility which has resulted from not getting his needs met satisfactorily. Therefore, given enough time, enthusiasm, which may be made up more out of blindness than insight, avoidance than confrontation, emptying a need instead of filling it, may very well lead to burnout in a given relationship. Enthusiasm may be motivated by burnout in another relationship or the result of not getting needs met satisfactorily in it. Things that once were not important, such as salary, working conditions, who will care for the children, when, where, and for how long, become very important.

4. What he is doing is what he deeply values. Jesus said, "For where your treasure is, there your heart will be also."[43]

5. His values are not contradictory. Paul said, "I do not know what I am doing. For what I want to do, I do not do, but what I hate I do."[44]

158

6. He is a person of depth whose values are realistic, adequate and clearly and precisely defined having given appropriate priorities to them. The Parable of the Sower, which could just as applicably be designated the Parable of the Soils speaks to this matter.

> Listen then to what the parable of the sower means: When anyone hears the message about the kingdom and does not understand it, the evil one comes and snatches away what was sown in his heart. This is the seed sown along the path. What was sown on rocky places is the man who hears the word and at once receives it with joy. But since he has no root, he lasts only a short time. When trouble or persecution comes because of the word, he quickly falls away. What was sown among the thorns is the man who hears the word, but the worries of this life and the deceitfulness of wealth choke it, making it unfruitful. But what was sown on good soil is the man who hears the word and understands it. He produces a crop, yielding a hundred, sixty or thirty times what was sown.[45]

7. He is a person who is not controlled by fear. The man who had one talent can teach a lesson at this point. Notice!

> Then the man who had received the one talent came. 'Master,' he said, 'I know that you are a hard man, harvesting where you have not sown and gathering where you have not scattered seed. So I was afraid and went out and hid your talent in the ground. See, here is what belongs to you.' His master replied, 'You wicked, lazy servant! So you knew that I harvest where I have not sown and gather where I have not scattered seed? Well, then, you should have put my money on deposit with the bankers, so that when I returned I would have received it back with interest.'[46]

8. He can accept the structure (system) and find professional and personal fulfillment within it.

9. He can accept his limitations. This includes his personal and professional limitations as well as the limitations the system and his client may impose upon him. Jesus illustrates this point. Notice!

> Jesus said to them, 'Only in his home town, among his relatives and in his own house is a prophet without honor.' He could not do any miracles there, except lay his hands on a few sick people and heal them. And he was amazed at their lack of faith. Then Jesus went around teaching from village to village.[47]

10. After recognizing and accepting the various limitations imposed upon him, he is still able to exert is power in a way that is to some degree helpful to the client and satisfying to himself. Paul said, "For God did not give us a spirit of timidity, but a spirit of power, of love, and of self-discipline."[48]

11. He is not pretentious. Solomon stated:

> Better to be a nobody and yet have a servant than pretend to be somebody and have no food.[49]

159

One man pretends to be rich, yet has nothing; another pretends to be poor, yet has great wealth.[50]

12. He knows whereof he speaks. Without ethical restrictions, it is relatively easy for a person to speak that which he does not really know and pretend to be what he is not. Paul said:

> Brothers, my heart's desire and prayer to God for the Israelites is that they may be saved. For I can testify about them that they are zealous for God, but their zeal is not based on knowledge. Since they disregarded the righteousness that comes from God and sought to establish their own, they did not submit to God's righteousness.[51]

> Some have wandered away from these and turned to meaningless talk. They want to be teachers of the law, but they do not know what they are talking about or what they so confidently affirm.[52]

Paul said of himself, "I speak the truth in Christ - I am not lying, my conscience confirms it in the Holy Spirit."[53] The Wise Man stated:

> It is not good to have zeal without knowledge, nor to be hasty and miss the way.[54]

> Gold there is, and rubies in abundance, but lips that speak knowledge are a rare jewel.[55]

STAGNATION, THE SECOND STAGE OF DISILLUSIONMENT

Enthusiasm is a condition in which one can easily get lost and is susceptible to becoming a fanatic because he is carried away by his feelings for a cause, principle or belief. It can be further characterized by high hopes, abundance of energy, and unrealistic expectations. Becoming over-identifed (with his spouse, child, a particular ministry, etc.), the enthusiastic person is excessive and inefficient in the use of his time and energy.

Stagnation, though, is the stage of disillusionment when disappointment gradually emerges and cannot be ignored. It is becoming aware, though painfully, that pious platitudes, superficial rituals, and romantic desires do not change the reality of life, make a spouse or child into who or what he is not. *It is easy for one to ignore reality when he is enthusiastic;* but when it emerges in stagnation, reality will not go away regardless of how determined one may be to ignore or avoid it. Obviously, it may take weeks, months, or years for stagnation to develop. As it sets in, one begins to see other aspects of his life and realizes he has more than one need. He becomes less interested in whatever or with whomever he was over-identified and more interested in such matters as pleasure, friends, family, financial security, and personal needs.

160

FRUSTRATION, THE THIRD STAGE OF DISILLUSIONMENT

Although treated separately, each of these stages are interwoven and do overlap. In real life an individual moves in and out, back and forth in them. Enthusiasm leads to stagnation and stagnation leads to frustration. Frustration comes as a result of one's not being able to realize his dreams and accomplish his goals. It results from time and again running up against the immovable barriers of his own limitations and those of the system in which he finds himself (his marriage, children, expertise or lack of it, limited finances, staff, administration, etc.). It results from ignoring his and the system's limitations instead of focusing on adjusting and learning to work within them. Frustration, then, is that feeling which one has when barriers continue to be in his way of accomplishing goals. This stage is where emotional, physical, and behavioral problems can occur.

APATHY, THE FOURTH STAGE OF DISILLUSIONMENT

Apathy is dull indifference, absence of feeling, or lack of interest. Paul said, "Let us not become weary in doing good, for at the proper time we will reap a harvest if we do not give up."[56] Although being tired or exhausted is inherent in the word *weary,* it also carries with it the idea to lose spirit or to become fainthearted. Jesus said to the church in Laodicea:

> I know your deeds, that you are neither cold nor hot. I wish your were either one or the other! So, because you are lukewarm – neither hot nor cold – I am about to spit you out of my mouth. You say, "I am rich; I have acquired wealth and do not need a thing." But you do not realize that you are wretched, pitiful, poor, blind and naked.[57]

In apathy a person usually rationalizes that *everything is okay.* He may drag through the duties of his ministry, the responsibilities of being a spouse or parent, but his heart is not in what he is doing because his commitments have little to no value to him now.

"REALISTIC" INTERVENTION IS NECESSARY TO BREAK THE CYCLE OF DISILLUSIONMENT

Realistic intervention begins with the *awareness that burnout does occur* as well *as what the stages of disillusionment are. Overidentification* with one person, group or activity to the neglect and exclusion of other needs and responsibilities leads to burnout. Although a person needs to accept his job, spouse, child, etc. for what it/he is, he can best do this when his other needs are also being met satisfactorily. There are different *networks* or *systems* in an individual's life such as family, church and vocation. In a healthy person the various systems function in some kind of balance. Maintaining a balance in one's relationships and responsibilities helps prevent burnout and provides strength for one when he is experiencing burnout in a given area. A balanced life not only helps to prevent burnout, it probably is the most effective intervention.

Realistic intervention can and should occur at any one of the four stags of disillusionment; it may be self-initiated or occur in response to an immediate frustration or threat. It may grow out of one's strength and the support and guidance he received from his peers, friends, family, and other important individuals in his life. It can result from increased education, relocation, better working and living conditions and a higher salary. It can be a temporary stop-gap or a real change. One should understand that stop-gap intervention or quick solutions neither solves any problems in the long run nor helps a person learn to meet this need in a realistic manner.

Intervention most often takes place (if at all) at the stage of frustration, when it is almost too late. Were it not for a person being so blind and having such a good time, enthusiasm would be the ideal stage for intervention to take place. During the stage of stagnation an individual has little energy and motivation to make realistic interventions. Apathy is the most severe and saddest, and is the hardest from which to bounce back. **It is the phase against which it is most difficult to intervene successfully because it is the most settled, the most deep seated and the one that takes the longest to arrive at and last the longest. It is very difficult for a counselor, spouse or parent to see and accept this fact because he is usually expecting immediate results. When such is not experienced, he tends to become more apathetic.**

Leaders often use *special series* on marriage and family living as a temporary stop-gap. The approach frequently used is to call in an *expert.* He usually focuses on getting the people *excited.* After the *excitement fades* individuals may be left either more disillusioned or suspended in mid air *waiting* for the *next special. Special series* should be used as a tool for learning and give one some substance not just excitement. Otherwise, they can contribute to a person becoming more apathetic in the long run.

FOOTNOTES

[1]Ecclesiates 7:8.

[2]See Deuteronomy 11:26, 28, 30; Joshua 24; Matthew 11:28-30; 23:37; Revelation 3:20.

[3]See 2 Peter 1:6; 1 Corinthians 9:27.

[4]Romans 12:3.

[5]Margaretha K. Bowers, *Conflicts of the Clergy* (New York: Thomas Nelson and Sons, 1963), p. vii. See also Paul E. Johnson, *Psychology of Pastoral Care* (New York: Abingdon Press, 1953) p. 45 and William J. Lederer and Don D. Jackson, *The Mirages of Marriage* (New York: W.W. Norton and Company, Inc. 1968) pp. 41-46.

[6]Bowers, *Conflicts of the Clergy,* p. vii. See also Lederer and Jackson, *The Mirages of Marriage,* p. 45.

[7]Bowers, *Conflicts of the Clergy,* p. vii.

[8]Carroll A. Wise. "The Call to the Ministry," *Pastoral Psychology,* IX, (December, 1958) pp. 9-17. See also Lederer and Jackson, *The Mirages of Marriage,* p. 45.

[9]Paul Tournier affirms that this may definitely be a reason for one entering the ministry. *The Strong and the Weak* trans. by Edwin Hudson, (Philadelphia: Westminister Press, 1963), p. 72. A number of people whom I have seen in marriage counseling got married and/or had children because of this fear.

[10]R. Lofton Hudson, "The Emotions of the Ministers," Pastoral Psychology, IX, (May, 1951), p. 37.

[11]Wise, "The Call to the Ministry", p. 13.

[12]Wayne C. Clark, *The Minister Looks at Himself* (Chicago: Judson Press, 1957), pp. 32, 33. Lederer and Jackson state: "Some individuals marry because of an unconscious desire to improve themselve." *The Mirages of Marriage,* p. 45.

[13]Wise, "The Call to the Ministry", p. 13.

[14]Clark, *The Minister Looks at Himself,* pp. 32, 33.

[15]Wise, "The Call to the Ministry," p. 14. See also Trounier, *The Strong and the Weak,* pp. 16, 17, 40, 57, 58, 64, 65. Lederer and Jackson state: "Romantic literature, tradition, and social hysteria have given marriage false values which the excited male and female often accept as true . . . They have been persuaded that love (which they cannot even define) automatically will make it possible to solve all problems." *The Mirages of Marriage,* p. 44. They also state that "the pressures and maneuverings of parents often push their children into premature and careless marriage." *Ibid.*

[16]See Luke 10:25-28; Romans 12:9; 1 Peter 1:22.

[17]Wise, "The Call to the Ministry," p. 12.

[18]*Ibid.*

[19]*Ibid.*

[20]Proverbs 20:5.

[21]Proverbs 20:25.

[22]Romans 7:15-17.

[23]Wise, "The Call to the Ministry," p. 14.

[24]Glen E. Whitlock, "The Choice of the Ministry as an Active or Passive Decision," *Pastoral Psychology,* XII, (March, 1961), p. 53.

[25]Wise, "The Call to the Ministry," p. 13.

[26]*Ibid.* See also: Samuel W. Blizzard, "The Parish Minister's Self-Image of His Master Role," *Pastoral Psychology,* XVII, (April, 1967), p. 17; Kenneth Crawford, "The Minister's Self-Image and Pastoral Counseling." *Pastoral Psychology,* XVII, (April, 1967), pp. 49-54.

[27]John P. Kildahl, "The Hazards of High Callings," *Pastoral Psychology,* XII, (March, 1961), p. 41.

[28]Hudson, "The Emotions of the Minister," p. 32.

[29]Wise, "The Call to the Ministry," p. 13.

[30]*Ibid.,* pp. 13, 14.

[31]*Ibid.,* p. 14.

[32]Jerry Edelwich with Archie Brodsky, *Burn-Out (New York: Human Sciences Press, 1980), p. 34. My sub-headings Enthusiasm, Stagnation, Frustration, and Apathy were borrowed from the authors.*

[33]Proverbs 14:15.

[34]Proverbs 14:12.

[35]Proverbs 16:2.

[36]Proverbs 21:2.

[37]Proverbs 19:20.

[38]Proverbs 19:27.

[39]**Proverbs 16:18.**

[40]Proverbs 13:10.

[41]Proverbs 11:2.

[42]Proverbs 18:12.

[43]**Matthew 6:21.**

[44]Romans 7:15.

[45]Matthew 13:18-23.

[46]Matthew 25:24-27.

[47]Mark 6:4-6.

[48]2 Timothy 1:7.

[49]Proverbs 12:9.

[50]Proverbs 13:7.

[51]Romans 10:1-3.

[52]1 Timothy 1:6,7.

[53]Romans 9:1.

[54]Proverbs 19:2.

[55]Proverbs 20:15.

[56]Galatians 6:9.

[57]Revelation 3:15-17.

Chapter 12

COUNSELING IS NOT A PANACEA

COUNSELING IS NOT "THE" ANSWER

Counseling is not a panacea. It is not for everyone at just anytime. Every leader is not an effective counselor. A person needs to have a sound and adequate counseling theory and proper training in the counseling process. Even training does not guarantee that he will be an effective counselor with all clients. Counselors are like ministers, they cannot be effective without adequate knowledge of theory. Knowledge alone does not guarantee one to be an effective pulpit speaker or counselor.

One should choose a counselor with caution. It is equally important that a counselor chooses his clients with caution. He needs to know what type of clients with which he works best and be comfortable in making referrals when it is appropriate. A counseling relationship is somewhat like marriage. If the two are suited for each other, committed to one another, and are willing to work openly, honestly, respectfully, and responsibly toward accomplishing certain goals then the relationship will more likely be a satisfactory one.

Since there are those who see counseling as a panacea they are offering it as a *quick cure all*. Currently there are leaders who see counseling as very simplistic, requiring little to no professional training and ongoing supervision of one's work with clients. Therefore, given enough time the blunders they make will confirm **the falsehood – "counseling should be viewed with suspicion and is probably bad for Christians". This approach will leave Christian leaders and their followers more apathetic regarding their personal, marital, and family difficulties and less motivated to seek help.**

COUNSELING IS ONE OF SEVERAL MINISTRIES

Christians have multiple ministries such as preaching, teaching, benevolence, etc. No ministry stands alone in the Scripture, although a person may focus primarily on a particular one. Since all ministries are interrelated, an individual is most effective when his particular ministry is interrelated with other ministries. Counseling is one ministry among several and does not stand alone. Christians need adequate and sound theory and appropriate relationships in which they can assimilate the theory into their persons and lives. In a technical sense there is an interrelation between teaching a Bible class and counseling. Therefore, a skilled counselor does not get lost in his arrogance. He understands in order for his counseling to be most effective it must be interrelated with other ministries.

ANXIETY AND ZEAL WITHOUT KNOWLEDGE ARE DANGEROUS

Some leaders in the church are anxious and concerned about what is happening in marriages and families. There was a time when leaders thought and taught that Christians did not have problems and being in the church automatically protected one's marriage and family from deterioration. Finally, thank God, leaders' eyes are being opened. What they are beginning to see is very frightening to them. Being anxious and zealous, they may be willing to accept quick and easy solutions to the problems.

Anyone who is sincere, zealous and not knowledgeable is easily frightened and can become gullible. Solomon said, "It is not good to have zeal without knowledge, nor to be hasty and miss the way."[1] It seems that leaders are continually looking for something simple, easy, and quick to solve complicated problems. There is no doubt that the problems facing couples and families today are serious and complex. Therefore, they will not be dealt with effectively by a person who has very little or no training, yet poses as an authority who is offering immediate solutions with little effort.

Counseling in the eyes of some leaders in the church today has moved from an attitude of *suspicion* to be *the answer to all problems of the church.* What is sad is **both positions are false.** They will lead to individuals becoming disillusioned and give up or simply start looking for other solutions. In the meantime Christian individuals, couples, and families will continue to suffer.

It seems to me if leaders really believe the home is in serious trouble, they would want to analyze why and seek help to find what is needed to really help troubled people. Leaders should not allow their anxiety and zeal to generate false hopes through offering "quick cures". Leaders need to understand they are contradicting themselves if they agree the problems of the home and family are

166

serious and complicated and then turn around and offer individuals quick, easy and simplistic solutions.

BEHAVIOR CHANGE IS NOT CHARACTER CHANGE

Sometimes leaders equate behavior change with character change. They are not the same. It is often said that a person can *act* himself into *feeling* better more easily and quickly than he can *feel* himself into *feeling better.* Even so, feeling better may not have anything to do with character change. To illustrate, to feel better after being drunk, an alcoholic frequently does things which have nothing to do with changing his character. He may simply be doing something (acting) to get rid of his hangover in order to feel better.

Thoughts, feelings and behavior are interrelated in a person being able to feel better. One of these may be more predominant at a given time. If a person is going to feel better, his thoughts, feelings, and behavior must all be involved. This can happen regardless of whether he is aware of the other components. Behavior which helps a feeling to change must be *related* to *that feeling* and in some way be an expression of that feeling. To illustrate, a woman may be depressed and decide to clean house. The cleaning of the house may be an expression of her hostility, which is part of the depression, as well as the need for her to feel some self-esteem, self-worth, a sense of accomplishment and belonging. In this case she is involved in thinking, doing and feeling although the focus may be on her behavior.

Sometimes a person has to experience feeling depressed, lonely, etc. before he can begin to feel better. This is certainly true with a person who is in grief. Getting related to self and others on a different level helps a person to feel better but requires the interrelation of thinking, feeling, and doing. Meaningful work is good therapy and certainly helps a person to feel he belongs, increase his sense of self-worth, and contributes to his meaning and purpose in life.

THE MOMENT OF AWARENESS IS NOT THE MOMENT OF SOLUTION

One educational fallacy widely held in the church (though not explicitly stated) is that the *moment* of awareness, memorization or especially insight of a *truth* is the moment one changes or solves his problems. This theory ignores the fact that a person came to be the way he is out of relationships and it takes ongoing relationships for him to assimilate new truths. A person's relationships need to be such that both individuals participate in giving and receiving intellectual and emotional truth. Since an individual develops character traits, deeply ingrained habits or styles in relationships over a period of years, it will likely take years of involvement in relationships to change them. Even then a person must have the ego strength, be sufficiently motivated, and persistent in appropriate ongoing intra-personal and interpersonal relationships. One such relationship may be with a psychotherapist.

INDIVIDUALS NEED "MORE" THAN CORRECT AND ADEQUATE INFORMATION

A number of leaders in the church seem to think that what individuals really need is correct and adequate information. The assumption is if they had this information, they could solve their own problems. There are a number of problems which accompany this view.

1. It is important to understand that a person may have needs of which he is unaware. Even if he is aware, he may not know how to get a particular need met on the desired level.

2. It assumes the advisor knows what a particular person needs at a given time and with clarity and precision, can articulate not only what a person needs, but how he may get those needs met.

3. It assumes that a particular individual wants his needs met in a certain way.

4. It assumes that a specific person has the ego strength and depth of motivation to persist long enough in order that a given need may be met satisfactorily.

5. It assumes that individuals want correct and adequate information. The Scripture is clear that not everyone does want the truth. Ezekiel was told:

> The people to whom I am sending you are obstinate and stubborn . . . . Do not rebel like that rebellious house; open your mouth and eat what I give you . . . . But the house of Israel is not willing to listen to you because they are not willing to listen to me, for the whole house of Israel is hardened and obstinate.[2]

The Christian counselor should "speak the truth in love"[3] and "be as shrewd as snakes and as innocent as doves."[4] The fact still remains though that some people do not wish to receive correct and adequate theory.

6. It assumes that having correct and adequate information guarantees the practice of it. Notice the fallacy! "For we also had the

gospel preached to us, just as they did; but the message they heard was of no value to them, because those who heard did not combine it with faith."[5]

7. It does not take into consideration the complicated human factors of being ready, receiving and assimilating intellectual or academic information.

a. Individuals not only have to understand what is said but they themselves must be intellectually and emotionally ready to hear and have the ego strength to endure the reception of certain information.

In helping individuals it becomes very important for the helper to understand it takes time to hear and act on certain information. When many of the disciples heard Jesus discussing the necessity of their being able to eat his flesh and drink his blood John records: "On hearing it, many of his disciples said, 'This is a hard teaching. Who can accept it?' "[6] Again Jesus said, "I have much more to say to you, more than you can bear."[7]

b. Helping a person to see that he is responsible for accepting or rejecting information is important to his assimilating of it. This may sound contrary to some current preaching but notice! Jesus asked:

'You do not want to leave too, do you?' Jesus asked the Twelve. Simon Peter answered him, 'Lord, to whom shall we go? You have the words of eternal life. We believe and know that you are the Holy One of God.'[8]

Moses stated:

See, I set before you today life and prosperity, death and destruction . . . .
This day I call heaven and earth as witnesses against you that I have set before you life and death, blessings and curses! Now choose life, so that you and your children may live and that you may love the Lord your God, listen to his voice, and hold fast to him. For the Lord is your life, and he will give you many years in the land he swore to your fathers, Abraham, Isaac and Jacob.[9]

Joshua stated:

But if serving the Lord seems undesirable to you, then choose for yourselves this day whom you will serve, whether the gods your forefathers served beyond the River, or the gods of the Amorites, in whose land you are living. But as for me and my household, we will serve the Lord.[10]

8. It does not take into consideration that learning which is more conducive to change is learning which comes from interacting (intellectually and emotionally) with the various members of the groups to which one belongs.

The strongest influences and the ones most difficult to change come from a person's primary group — his family. Solomon said:

> Discipline your son, for in that there is hope; do not be a willing party to his death.[11]

> Train up a child in the way he should go and when he is old he will not turn from it.[12]

Paul said:

> I have been reminded of your sincere faith, which lived in your grandmother Lois and in your mother Eunice and, I am persuaded, now lives in you also.[13]

A person's early peer relationships also has a significant influence on his character development. Like in his family, the earlier the influences the more complicated and difficult it is for him to change. Solomon said: "My son, if sinners entice you, do not give into them."[14] Paul said: "Do not be misled: 'bad company corrupts good character'."[15] It is an established fact that the group to which one belongs directly influences what he becomes. The nature of the group, the length of time he felt he belonged to the group, the age at which he became a member of it, and the frequency with which the group met are determinants in what influences and their depths have on an individual.

Another group which has the potential to have a significant influence on a person is the church or body of Christ. The Scriptures set forth this fact with clarity. Paul said:

> For by the grace given to me I say to every one of you: Do not think of yourself more highly than you ought, but rather think of yourself with sober judgment, in accordance with the measure of faith God has given you. Just as each of us has one body with many members, and these members do not all have the same function, so in Christ we who are many form one body, and each member belongs to all the others.[16]

He also said:

> The body is a unit, though it is made up of many parts; and though all its parts are many, they form one body. So it is with Christ . . . .
>
> Now the body is not made up of one part but of many. If the foot should say, 'Because I am not a hand, I do not belong to the body,' it would not for that reason cease to be a part of the body. And if the ear should say 'Because I am not an eye, I do not belong to the body,' it would not for that reason cease to be part of the body. If the whole body were an eye, where would the sense of hearing be? If the whole body were an ear, where would the sense of smell be? But in fact God has arranged the parts in the body, every one of them, just as he wanted them to be. If they were all one part, where would the body be? As it is, there are many parts, but one body.
>
> The eye cannot say to the hand,'I don't need you!' And the head cannot say to the feet, 'I don't need you!' On the contrary, those parts of the body that seem to be weaker are indispensable, and the parts that we think are less

170

honorable we treat with special honor. And the parts that are unpresentable are treated with special modesty, while our presentable parts need no **special treatment. But God has combined the members of the body and has** given greater honor to the parts that lacked it, so that there should be no division in the body, but that its parts should have equal concern for each other. If one part suffers, every part suffers with it; if one part is honored, every part rejoices with it.

Now you are the body of Christ, and each one of you is a part of it.[17]

Again Paul stated:

Consequently, you are no longer foreigners and aliens, but fellow citizens with God's people and members of God's household, built on the foundation of the apostles and prophets, with Christ Jesus himself as the chief cornerstone. In him the whole building is joined together and rises to become a holy temple in the Lord. And in him you too are being built together to become a dwelling in which God lives by his spirit.[18]

Finally Paul said:

Therefore, encourage one another and build each other up, just as in fact you are doing.[19]

The church can be and sometimes is more in the way of a person's growth than an instrument to help him grow. This I have learned from my experience as a therapist and minister. It is certainly not a compliment but a fact of reality. If this is the case, the church cannot change until she faces reality. I do not know all the reasons why the church gets in the way of its members' growth, but suggest that some are:

a. Leaders have not thoroughly studied and, therefore, do not understand the importance of utilizing group dynamics as a means of growth.

b. Not understanding the nature of resistance as a part of the growth process, leaders have either tried to avoid it or confront it inappropriately. One common way leaders have attempted to meet resistance has been through becoming more rigid and authoritarian which tends to either create an open fight resulting in a church split or the more passive individuals just leave.

c. One of the ways in which leaders tend to deal with resistance to growth in troubled families is creating guilt through simplistic lectures and sermons.

Just giving correct and adequate information ignores the fact that one is formed and/or deformed, humiliated and/or esteemed in relationships. What has taken years to develop cannot be changed quickly without appropriate ongoing relationships, even though one may be subjected to correct and adequate information. Jesus spent more than three years with Judas in an ongoing day-to-day relationship and Judas ended up betraying him. Therefore, leaders who follow Jesus' example cannot *tell somebody what to do* and expect appropriate change to automatically result. Brief, serious reflection quickly reveals the arrogance and haughtiness of such an attitude. Solomon stated:

> When pride comes, then comes disgrace, but with humility comes wisdom.[20]
>
> Pride only breeds quarrels, but wisdom is found in those who take advice.[21]
>
> Pride goes before destruction, a haughty spirit before a fall.[22]

Leaders often fall and disgrace themselves because of arrogance, expressed through thinking that a few *how to* courses on techniques, with little to no introspection and struggling with themselves and their motives for counseling will bring disgrace to themselves and counseling as a biblical ministry. It is arrogant to ask someone else to do what one has not been and is not willing to do. Why should counselors ask their clients to look and struggle with their thoughts, feelings, behaviors, and motives if they have been and/are unwilling to struggle with themselves, their marriages and families.

The Making of a Counselor

A person does not become an effective counselor overnight. Counseling is an art or skill which must be learned through study. An individual who is an effective counselor demonstrates considerable skill in three areas.

1. Knowledge and appropriate use of self in a counseling relationship.

2. Knowledge of client obtained through studying psychology, history taking and the counseling process.

3. Understanding and assimiliation of sound counseling theory for relating effectively to the client.

I see the above three areas as being interrelated and they help to balance each other. A part of what concerns me is that individuals may know very little or a great deal about their client and counseling theory, but know nearly nothing about themselves and the counseling process. It is a basic assumption of mine that regardless of one's theory, he counsels out of himself whether he knows it or not. It seems to me if a person really desires to be an effective counselor, he would want to know himself and how he relates to others. I get the impression from some who call themselves counselors that they are not willing to take the time, and go through the pain of discovering themselves and how they function with others. I think those of us who call ourselves counselors should take Paul seriously when he said:

> You, then, who teach others, do you not teach yourself? You who preach against stealing, do you steal? you who say that people should not commit adultery, do you commit adultery? You who abhor idols, do you rob temples? You who brag about the law, do you dishonor God by breaking the law?[23]

I am of the opinion that an effective counselor is *made not born.* What appears to *come naturally* is largely the result of years of training — training in the laboratory of life. It is the process of assimiliating *what* and *how* one saw with this eyes, heard with his ears, and understood with his heart as he was growing up accompanied with sound, academic and clinical training after he has chronologically matured. Therefore, there are likely several individuals and different experiences which significantly influence a person to become a counselor, as well as how effective he might function as one.

FOOTNOTES

[1]Proverbs 19:2.
[2]Ezekiel 2:4, 8; 3:7.
[3]Ephesians 4:15.
[4]Matthew 10:16.
[5]Hebrews 4:2.
[6]John 6:60.
[7]John 16:12.
[8]John 6:67-69.
[9]Deuteronomy 30:15, 19, 20.
[10]Joshua 24:15.
[11]Proverbs 19:18.
[12]Proverbs 22:6.
[13]2 Timothy 1:5.
[14]Proverbs 1:10.
[15]1 Corinthians 15:33.
[16]Romans 12:3-5.
[17]1 Corinthians 12:12, 14-27.
[18]Ephesians 2:19-22.
[19]1 Thessalonians 5:11.
[20]Proverbs 11:2.
[21]Proverbs 13:10.
[22]Proverbs 16:18.
[23]Romans 2:21-23.